Handball Practice 14 – Interaction of back position players with the pivot – Shifting, Screening, and Using the Russian Screen

handball-uebungen.de
Trainingseinheiten und Übungen für Ihr Training!

Table of contents:

Introduction

Publishing information
1st English edition released on 16 Apr 2018
German original edition released on 04 Dec 2017

Published by DV Concept
Editors, design, and layout: Jörg Madinger, Elke Lackner
Proofreading and English translation: Nina-Maria Nahlenz

ISBN: 978-3-95641-205-9

This publication is listed in the catalogue of the **German National Library**. Please refer to http://dnb.de for bibliographic data.

Handball Practice 14 – Interaction of back position players with the pivot – Shifting, Screening, and Using the Russian Screen

handball-uebungen.de
Trainingseinheiten und Übungen für Ihr Training!

Introduction

Dear reader

Thank you for choosing a book of the handball-uebungen.de training guide series.

The small group play of the back position players and the pivot is an important offense element in almost each age group. The basics of interacting with the pivot should already be established in the training of youth teams. Positioning and screening play an important role here. The first three training units in the book provide different options of interacting with the pivot.

With increasing age, the space for team play gets smaller. This leads to more challenging running paths for the back position players and higher requirements for the pivot's screening.

Particularly in adult teams, the physical characteristics of the pivot play a role, too. The last training unit focuses on achieving positional advantages by positioning the physically stronger pivot next to a physically weaker defending player (mismatch).

The courses of each training unit are set up step by step and have numerous supporting notes.

Handball Practice 14 – Interaction of back position players with the pivot – Shifting, Screening, and Using the Russian Screen

handball-uebungen.de
Trainingseinheiten und Übungen für Ihr Training!

This book contains the following training units:

TU 1: Individual training for the pivot – Pushing through the defense with the Russian screen (TU 200) (★★)

The objective of this training unit is to improve the positioning of the pivot. After warm-up and a short game, there will be a goalkeeper warm-up shooting from the pivot position. The players practice the pivot's pushing through the defense in an individual offense exercise. Afterwards, there are two exercises in which the players practice positioning and the Russian screen in small groups against defensive and semi-offensive defense players. The players should implement the variants in the closing game.

TU 2: Pivot – Achieving positional advantages in small-group team play (TU 210) (★★)

The objective of this training unit is to improve the positioning of the pivot. Following warm-up and a short game, the players practice passing to the pivot under difficult conditions and with different passing variants during the ball familiarization and goalkeeper warm-up shooting phases. Afterwards, there will be an individual exercise regarding the pivot's screening followed by two small group exercises in which the interaction with the back position and wing players will be practiced. In a closing game, the players should implement what they practiced before.

TU 3: Improving the interaction of back position players with the pivot (TU 271) (★★★)

The objective of this training unit is to practice the interaction of a back position player with the pivot. Following warm-up and a running coordination exercise, the players prepare for the running moves in the back positions during the ball familiarization phase. After the goalkeeper warm-up shooting, there will be three offense exercises in which the players further develop the team play step by step. In a 4-on-4 game, the players should implement what they practiced before.

TU 4: Small group game: Piston movement / countermovement of the back position players and interaction with the pivot (TU 205) (★★)

This training unit focuses on the interaction of the back position players with each other regarding piston movement/countermovement and passing to the pivot. Following warm-up, the back position players take the first methodical step regarding the interaction with the pivot during the ball familiarization phase. During the goalkeeper warm-up shooting and a subsequent offense exercise, the players practice the piston movement/countermovement which should result in a shot. In the following two small group exercises, the players stepwise further develop their piston movement/countermovement and the interaction with the pivot. The final exercise combines the different elements that the players practiced before with an initial action and creative continuous playing.

Handball Practice 14 – Interaction of back position players with the pivot – Shifting, Screening, and Using the Russian Screen

handball-uebungen.de
Trainingseinheiten und Übungen für Ihr Training!

TU 5: Acting against the defending wing position player with a physically stronger pivot (TU 363) (★★★★)

This training unit focuses on simple initial actions in order to gain positional advantage by having a physically stronger pivot play against a physically weaker defense player on the wing positions. The warm-up phase focuses on coordination. Afterwards, the players practice the first steps of the subsequent team play during the ball familiarization and goalkeeper warm-up shooting phases. The three subsequent offense exercises consist of the preparation and the final 1-on-1 play to get the pivot into a good shooting position. A closing game completes this training unit.

Training unit requirements:

★	Simple requirement (all youth and adult teams)
★★	Intermediate requirement (youth teams under 15 years of age and adult teams)
★★★	Higher requirement (youth teams under 17 years of age and adult teams)
★★★★	Highest requirements (competitive area)

Handball Practice 14 – Interaction of back position players with the pivot – Shifting, Screening, and Using the Russian Screen

handball-uebungen.de
Trainingseinheiten und Übungen für Ihr Training!

1. Structuring a training unit

The focus of the training should run like a red thread through the entire unit. It is advisable to follow the basic timescale below:
- Approx. 10 (15) minutes – warm-up.
- Approx. 20 (30) minutes – basic exercises (2 to 3 exercises max. plus goalkeeper warm-up shooting).
- Approx. 20 (30) minutes – basic play.
- Approx. 10 (15) minutes – target play.

1st timescale for a 60-minute training unit / 2nd timescale in brackets for a 90-minute training unit.

Warm-up practices
- Opening of the training unit: It may be advisable to start the training unit with a ritual (get together in a circle, exchanging high-fives) and to explain the contents and the objectives of the training unit to the players.
- Basic warm-up: Jogging, activation of blood circulation and the musculoskeletal system.
- Stretching/strengthening/mobilization: Preparing the body for the physical stress of the training unit.
- Short games: These should already focus on the objective of the training unit.

Basic exercises
- Ball familiarization (focused on the objective of the training unit).
- Goalkeeper warm-up shooting (focused on the objective of the training unit).
- Individual technique and tactics training.
- Technique and tactics training in small groups.

In general, the running and passing paths are predefined during the basic exercises (you may increase and vary the requirements during the course of the exercise).

Additional information on basic exercise
- Each player should do the drill (switch quickly).
- Very frequent repetitions.
- The players should rotate or do the drill on both sides simultaneously / slightly delayed to avoid long waiting periods.
- Practice individually (1-on-1 to 2-on-2 max.).
- Add additional tasks/drills, if applicable (to make the exercise more complex).

Handball Practice 14 – Interaction of back position players with the pivot – Shifting, Screening, and Using the Russian Screen

handball-uebungen.de
Trainingseinheiten und Übungen für Ihr Training!

Basic play

Most of all, the basic play differs from the basic exercise in such a way that now there are several **options for action** (decisions). The player(s) should realize the respective options and make the correct decision. Here, the players practice decision-making in particular.

- The players should now implement what they practiced during the basic exercises under **competitive conditions**.
- Working with alternative actions – practicing the decision-making process.
- The players should repeat the drill frequently and try out different actions.
- Working in small groups (3-on-3 to 4-on-4 max.).

Target play

- The players now implement what they practice before in free play. To increase their motivation, you may award additional points or additional attacks for correct implementation.
- In the target play, the players implement what they practiced before (5-on-5, 6-on-6).

Depending on the contents and the objectives of the training unit, you may have to slightly adjust the timescales of the basic exercise and basic play.

Handball Practice 14 – Interaction of back position players with the pivot – Shifting, Screening, and Using the Russian Screen

handball-uebungen.de
Trainingseinheiten und Übungen für Ihr Training!

Choose topic of training unit:
➜ Red thread

Warm up:
Time:
-   approx. 10 (15) minutes
Practices:
-   "Playful warm-up"
-   Games
-   Coordination runs
-   (Stretching and strengthening)

Basic exercise:
Time:
-   approx. 20 (30) minutes
Characteristics:
-   Individual/Small groups
Practices:
-   Exact instructions re. course of the exercise
-   Variants with exact instructions re. the course
-   From simple to complex
-   No waiting periods for players

Basic play:
Time:
-   approx. 20 (30) minutes
Characteristics:
-   Small groups
Practices:
-   Exact instructions re. course
-   Competition

Target play:
Time:
-   approx. 10 (15) minutes
Characteristics:
-   Team play (small groups)
Practices:
-   Free play with the contents of the basic exercise and basic play
-   Competition

Handball Practice 14 – Interaction of back position players with the pivot – Shifting, Screening, and Using the Russian Screen

handball-uebungen.de
Trainingseinheiten und Übungen für Ihr Training!

2. Preparatory exercises for the pivot

The training units in this book focus on the interaction of the back position players with the pivot and in particular on screening.

During the preparatory exercises, the players repeat certain individual movements for the pivot's playing; however, these movements are considered as a precondition to some extent.

The following individual offense exercises for the pivot may be done in preparation for the training units.

No. P1	Series of shots for the pivot 1	2	★
Equipment required:	2 cones, ball box with sufficient number of handballs		

Course:

- runs an "8 path" around the cones, receives a pass from into his running path (A), and shoots from the pivot position (B).
- Afterwards, immediately starts running the "8 path" and the course starts over (C).

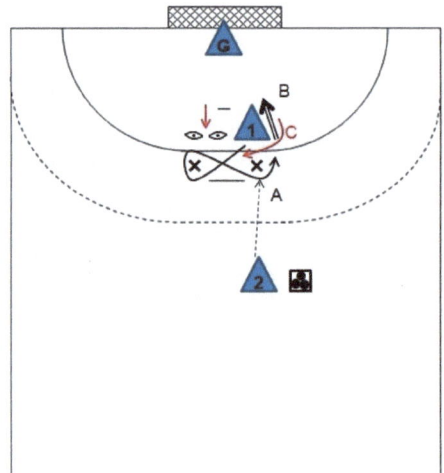

Repetitions:

- 10 shots in competition with a second/third pivot player. Who has scored most often after 10 shots?

should do the running movement around the cones at full speed.

Handball Practice 14 – Interaction of back position players with the pivot – Shifting, Screening, and Using the Russian Screen

handball-uebungen.de
Trainingseinheiten und Übungen für Ihr Training!

No. P2	Series of shots for the pivot 2	2	★★
Equipment required:	2 small vaulting boxes, 1 cone, sufficient number of handballs		

Setting:

- Position two small vaulting boxes as shown in the figure, with the upholstered side facing inside.
- Define the running path with a cone.

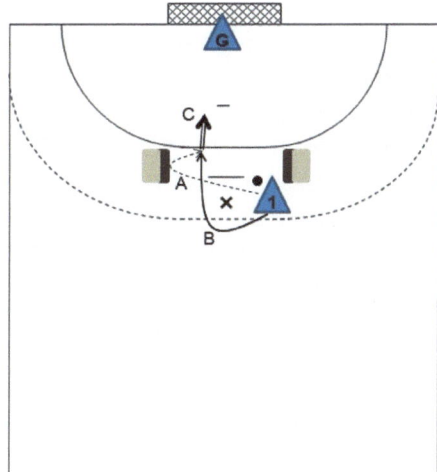

Course:

- ![1] throws his ball at the small vaulting box (A), runs around the cone (B), picks up the ball again, and shoots at the goal (C).

- In the next course, ![1] starts from the other side.

- The players may do the course with a second (third) pivot alternately.

Variants:

- The players should play a bounce pass (simpler) or a direct pass (more difficult) against the small vaulting box.

- One player plays the pass (A), while ![1] does several preparatory exercises:
  - o Jumping jacks on the spot.
  - o Somersault on a small gym mat.
  - o Juggle with three balls.

Handball Practice 14 – Interaction of back position players with the pivot – Shifting, Screening, and Using the Russian Screen

handball-uebungen.de
Trainingseinheiten und Übungen für Ihr Training!

No. P3	Win a back-bouncing ball and shoot subsequently	3	★★
Equipment required:	1 kickback rebounder, sufficient number of handballs		

Setting:

- Position a kickback rebounder next to the goal.

Course:

- **1** stands with his back turned to the goal.

- **2** throws a ball at the kickback rebounder (A).

- As soon as the ball has left the hand of **2**, **1** turns around, tries to rate (C) and win the back-bouncing ball (B).

- If **1** succeeds in winning the ball, he may shoot at the goal (D).

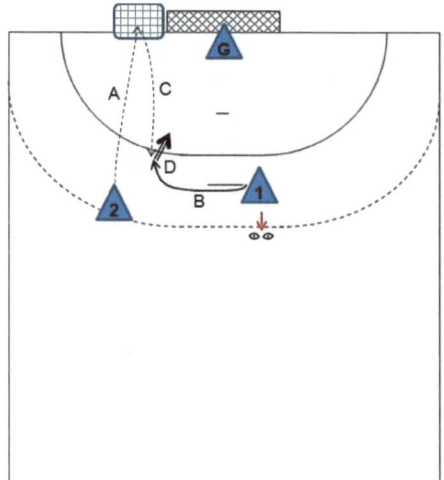

Variants:

- **1** does jumping jacks on the spot.

- **1** does a somersault on a small gym mat and tries to win the ball afterwards. **2** throws the ball at the kickback rebounder while **1** does the somersault.

⚠ Also do the course on the right side.

Handball Practice 14 – Interaction of back position players with the pivot – Shifting, Screening, and Using the Russian Screen

handball-uebungen.de
Trainingseinheiten und Übungen für Ihr Training!

No. P4	Fast adjustment and winning the ball	5	★★
Equipment required:	1 cone, 1 bib, sufficient number of handballs		

Setting:

- Define the starting position of the pivot.

- 🔺2 holds a bib in the beginning.

Course:

- 🔺1 starts at the cone.

- 🔺2 throws the bib in the air (A).

- This is the sign for 🔺1 to move away from the cone and to catch the bib before it reaches the ground (B).

- As soon as 🔺1 has caught the bib, 🔺3 starts to dribble on the left back position (C).

- 🔺1 throws the bib back to 🔺2, runs around the cone (D), and tries to win the ball, which 🔺3 throws around 🟢1's body into the gap (E).

- 🔺1 shoots at the goal (F).

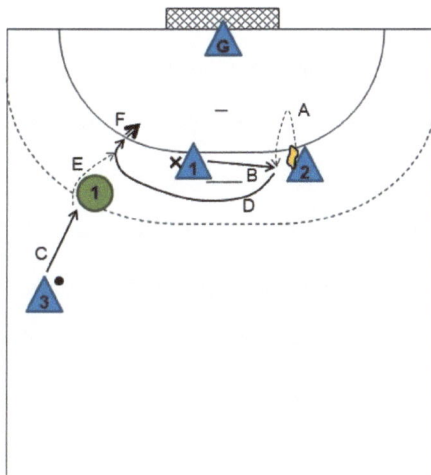

⚠ Adjust the running path (D) and the timing of the pass (E) to the players' level of performance.

Handball Practice 14 – Interaction of back position players with the pivot – Shifting, Screening, and Using the Russian Screen

handball-uebungen.de
Trainingseinheiten und Übungen für Ihr Training!

No. P5	**Fast adjustment and pushing through the defense 1**	5	★★
Equipment required:	Sufficient number of handballs		

Course:

- 🔺1 stands with his back turned to 🟢1 and receives a pass from 🔺3 (A).

- 🔺1 catches the ball with one hand while resisting against 🟢1's pressure and passes the ball back to 🔺3 (B).

- With the return pass, 🔺2 rolls a ball into the 9-meter zone (C).

- 🔺1 runs to the ball (D) and picks it up.

- 🟢1 runs along with him (E) and tries to prevent 🔺1 from breaking through towards the goal, once 🔺1 has taken up the ball.

- 🔺1 tries to break through (F) and shoot at the goal (G).

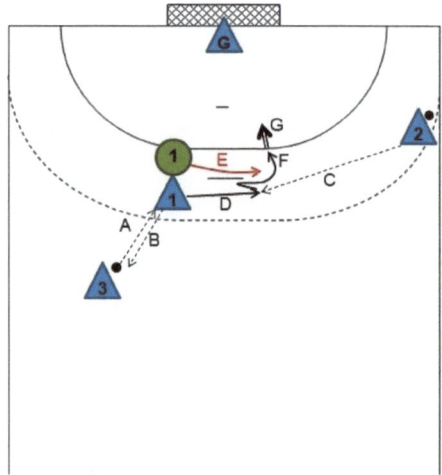

⚠️ 🟢1 should start his defense action only after 🔺1 has taken up the ball. The players should allow the initial pass (A) and the winning of the ball (D).

⚠️ In the beginning, 🟢1 should defend with an intensity of 80% of maximum. The pressure will be increased during the further course of the exercise.

Handball Practice 14 – Interaction of back position players with the pivot – Shifting, Screening, and Using the Russian Screen

handball-uebungen.de
Trainingseinheiten und Übungen für Ihr Training!

No. P6	Fast adjustment and pushing through the defense 2	6	★★

Equipment required:	2 small gym mats, ball box with sufficient number of handballs

Setting:
-   Position two small gym mats as shown in the figure.

Course:
-   **1** starts the drill and stands behind **1** (A).
-   **3** runs towards **1** with the ball and "pushes" it through around **1**'s body to **1** (B).

⚠️ **!** **1** should act defensively and allow the pass.

-   **1** picks up the ball and shoots at the goal (C).
-   Immediately after the shot, **1** does a somersault on the small gym mat (D), runs back over the mat, receives the second ball from **3** (E), and eventually shoots at the goal (F).
-   Repeat the course with **2** and **3** (G).
-   Once **2** has finished his series of shots, **1** repeats the drill one more time; afterwards, it is **2**'s turn (**1** and **2** each shoot 4 times in total).
-   Afterwards, the players each move to the next position and repeat the drill.

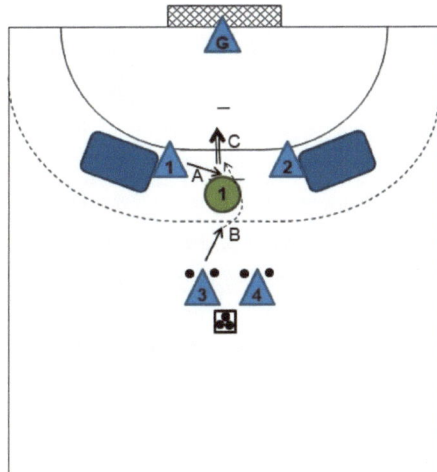

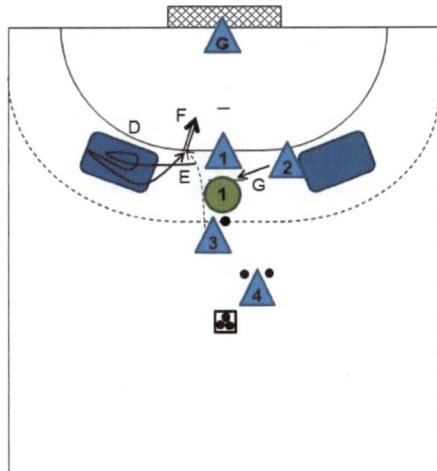

Overall course:
-   Each player does the drill four times (= 16 shots).

Handball Practice 14 – Interaction of back position players with the pivot – Shifting, Screening, and Using the Russian Screen

handball-uebungen.de
Trainingseinheiten und Übungen für Ihr Training!

3. Roles/tasks of the coach

It is mainly the personality and the behavior of the coach that makes the training a success. Therefore, it is important to observe certain behavioral rules to guarantee a successful training. The coach's social skills have an impact as important as his expertise. Especially when training youth teams, the coach serves as a role model and may influence the development of the young players.

A coach should:
- describe the training and its objectives to his team at the beginning of the training unit
- always speak loud and clear
- talk from such a position that all players can hear his instructions and corrections
- recognize and correct mistakes and give advice when correcting
- mainly correct what is part of the training objective
- point out and compliment on individual progress (give the player self-confidence)
- support and permanently challenge the players
- always be a role model – during training and games, but also outside the court
- come to training and games well-prepared and in a timely manner

Especially when training youth teams:
- the coach should react to different physical preconditions.
- motivate the players to hang in, even if they face certain difficulties in the beginning.

Handball Practice 14 – Interaction of back position players with the pivot – Shifting, Screening, and Using the Russian Screen

handball-uebungen.de
Trainingseinheiten und Übungen für Ihr Training!

4. Training units

TU 1:	Individual training for the pivot – Pushing through the defense with the Russian screen		★★	90

Opening part		Main part		
X	Warm-up/Stretching	X	Offense/Individual		Jumping power
	Running exercise	X	Offense/Small groups		Sprint contest
X	Short game		Offense/Team		Goalkeeper
	Coordination		Offense/Series of shots		**Final part**
	Coordination run		Defense/Individual		
	Strengthening		Defense/Small groups	X	Closing game
	Ball familiarization		Defense/Team		Final sprint
X	Goalkeeper warm-up shooting		Athletics		
			Endurance		

Key:

✖ Cone

△1 Attacking player

●1 Defense player

▣ Ball box

Equipment required:
➔ 5 cones, ball box with sufficient number of handballs, whistle

Description:
The objective of this training unit is to improve the positioning of the pivot. After warm-up and a short game, there will be a goalkeeper warm-up shooting from the pivot position. The players practice the pivot's pushing through the defense in an individual offense exercise. Afterwards, there are two exercises in which the players practice positioning and the Russian screen in small groups against defensive and semi-offensive defense players. The players should implement the variants in the closing game.

The training unit consists of the following key exercises:
- Warm-up/Stretching (individual exercise: 10 minutes/total time: 10 minutes)
- Short game (10/20)
- Goalkeeper warm-up shooting (10/30)
- Offense/Individual (15/45)
- Offense/Small groups (20/65)
- Offense/Small groups (10/75)
- Closing game (15/90)

Training unit total time: 90 minutes

Handball Practice 14 – Interaction of back position players with the pivot – Shifting, Screening, and Using the Russian Screen

handball-uebungen.de
Trainingseinheiten und Übungen für Ihr Training!

No.: 1-1	Warm-up/Stretching	10	10

Setting:

- Position several cones outside of the 9-meter zone.

Course:

- The players crisscross through the 9-meter zone while dribbling the ball (A).
- While doing this, they perform different running and dribbling variants (dribbling with arm rotation, hopping and dribbling, dribbling with the right/left hand alternately etc.).
- Upon the coach's whistle, the players make pairs, take each other by the hand, run together around one of the cones, and run back to the 9-meter zone (B). Both players dribble their ball during the hand-in-hand run.
- The players who arrive the 9-meter zone last and the players who didn't find a running partner must do 10 quick jumping jacks. Repeat the drill afterwards.

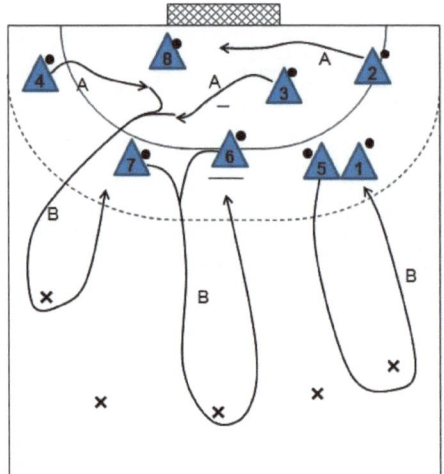

The players perform stretching exercises together.

Handball Practice 14 – Interaction of back position players with the pivot – Shifting, Screening, and Using the Russian Screen

handball-uebungen.de
Trainingseinheiten und Übungen für Ihr Training!

No.: 1-2	Short game	10	20

Course:

- Two players try to catch the other players (A).
- The player who is holding the ball and the player who held the ball last must not be caught.
- Hence, the fleeing players always must pass the ball to the player who is currently in danger of being caught (B).
- Once a player has been caught, he becomes the catcher.

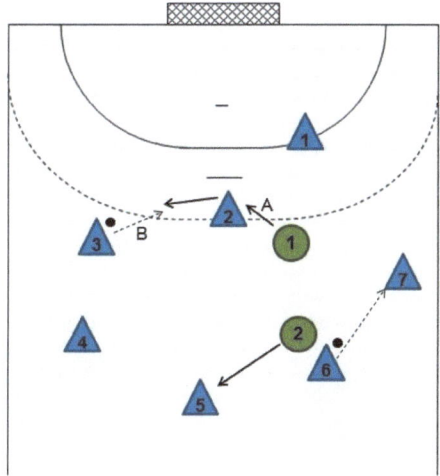

Important:

- There must be as much balls in the game as there are catchers.
- Tag the catchers (let them carry a bib, for example).

Handball Practice 14 – Interaction of back position players with the pivot – Shifting, Screening, and Using the Russian Screen

handball-uebungen.de
Trainingseinheiten und Übungen für Ihr Training!

No.: 1-3	Goalkeeper warm-up shooting	10	30

Setting:

- The players each hold a ball and stand along the 6-meter line. One player is the wing player (and stands at the 9-meter line).

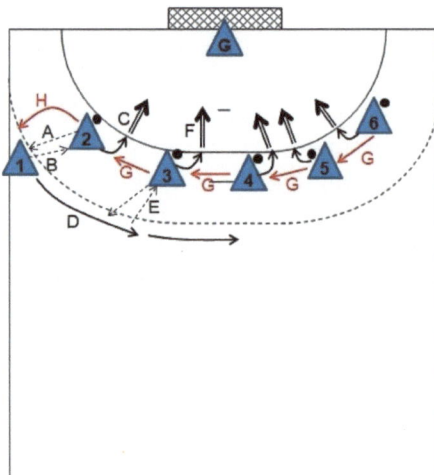

Course:

- ▲2 passes to ▲1 (A), receives a return pass (B), turns around at the 6-meter line and shoots at the goal (C) as instructed (hands, top, bottom).

- Immediately after ▲1 has played the return pass to ▲2 (B), ▲1 runs along the 9-meter line (D),

  plays a double pass with ▲3 (E), who also turns around and shoots (F), then plays a double pass with ▲4 etc. until ▲1 has played a double pass with each player and everyone has shot at the goal.

- After the shot, the players pick up their ball and move to the next position on the left (G). ▲1 moves to the 6-meter line on the right wing position and ▲2 plays the double passes in the next round (H).

- And so on.

⚠ The players should play the double passes in a quick and safe manner, so that the shooting players can shoot immediately after each other and hence provide a series of shots for the goalkeeper.

⚠ The players standing at the 6-meter line may choose the direction in which they turn. After several courses, the players should change the direction in which they turn, if applicable.

Handball Practice 14 – Interaction of back position players with the pivot – Shifting, Screening, and Using the Russian Screen

handball-uebungen.de
Trainingseinheiten und Übungen für Ihr Training!

No.: 1-4	Offense/Individual	15	45

Setting:

- Three defense players stand at the 6-meter line.
- Provide a sufficient number of handballs.

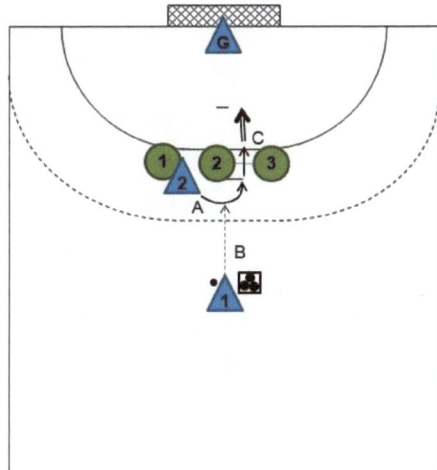

Figure 1

Basic course:

- The pivot (2) does eight actions in a row (four actions on each side). Switch tasks afterwards (new pivot, defense players, feeder).

Course 1 (figure 1):

- The defense players 2 and 3 stand face-to-face holding hands.

- 2 starts from the left side, runs around 2 (A), receives a pass from 1 into his running path (B), jumps through the gap between 2 and 3, and shoots (C).

- 2 breaks through the barrier (i.e. the arms of 2 and 3). The two defense players hold hands loosely so that they can let go at the time of the break-through. However, they do not let go before 2 has touched them.

- Afterwards, 2 turns around, holds hands with 1, and 2 starts for the next shot from the other side.

Handball Practice 14 – Interaction of back position players with the
pivot – Shifting, Screening, and Using the Russian Screen

handball-uebungen.de
Trainingseinheiten und Übungen für Ihr Training!

Course 2 (figure 2):

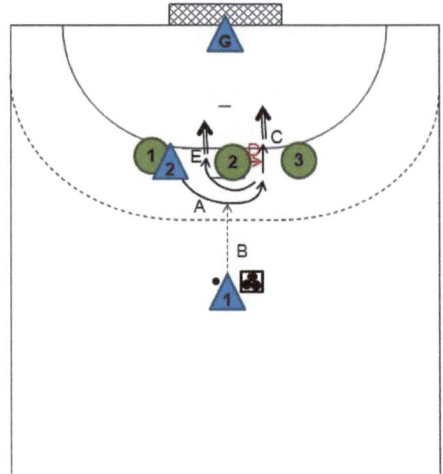

Figure 2

- The defense players leave a larger gap than in course 1 and do not hold hands anymore.

- **2** starts from the left side, runs around **2** (A), receives a pass from **1** into his running path (B), and tries to jump through the gap between **2** and **3** (C).

- If **2** moves towards **3** and closes the gap on this side (D), **2** moves around **2** and shoots on the left side of **2** (E).

- **2** starts the next round on the right side.

⚠ The outer defense players hold their positions; only **2** may close the gap.

⚠ **2** should move dynamically at the 6-meter line and jump through the gaps courageously.

Handball Practice 14 – Interaction of back position players with the pivot – Shifting, Screening, and Using the Russian Screen

handball-uebungen.de
Trainingseinheiten und Übungen für Ihr Training!

No.: 1-5	Offense/Small groups	20	65

Setting:

- Divide the court in two halves (right half, left half) with a cone.

Course 1 (figure 1):

- ◢1 passes to ◢3 (A), runs a curve towards the center (B), and receives a return pass (C).

- As soon as ◢1 plays the initial pass to ◢3, ②2 moves to the 6-meter line and screens off ①1 at the inner side.

- ◢1 must decide:

  o If ②2 remains defensive,

  ◢1 shoots from the back position (not shown in the figure).

  o If ②2 makes a step forward towards ◢1 (D), ◢1 plays a pass into the gap behind ②2 (E), to ◢2, who leaves the screening position and shoots at the goal (F).

- After the action, ②2 moves to the other half of the court (G). ◢4 starts the course on the other side (H and J) with ◢5 as the pivot.

Figure 1

Course 2 (figure 2):

- The initial action of course 1 (A to C) remains the same; however, now the players interact with the pivot on the other side.

- ◢1 must decide:

  o If ②2 remains defensive, ◢1 shoots from the back position (not shown in the figure).

  o If ②2 makes a step forward towards ◢1 (D), ◢5 runs into the gap (E), receives a pass from ◢1 into his running path (F), and eventually shoots at the goal (G).

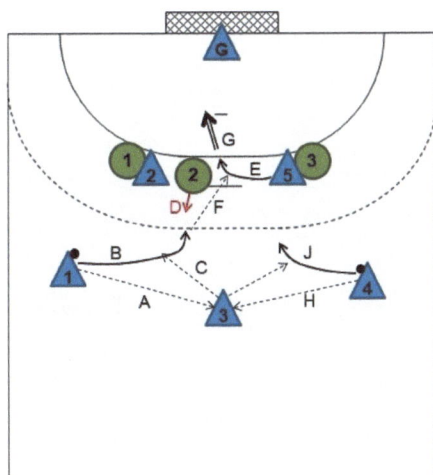

Figure 2

Handball Practice 14 – Interaction of back position players with the pivot – Shifting, Screening, and Using the Russian Screen

handball-uebungen.de
Trainingseinheiten und Übungen für Ihr Training!

- After the action, ② moves to the other half of the court. ④ starts the course on the other side (H and J) with ② as the pivot.

⚠ The pivots should keep screening for as long as possible on the respective inner side and leave the screening position as late as possible.

⚠ The defense players increase the pressure during the course of the exercise, so that the pivot must work hard in order to hold his position for the shot.

⚠ In both courses, the pivots switch positions after several rounds and also do the course on the respective other side.

No.: 1-6	Offense/Small groups	10	75

Setting:
- Divide the court in two halves (right half, left half) with a cone.

Course:

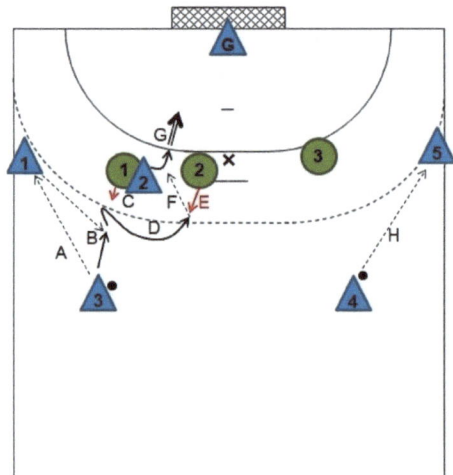

- ③ passes to ① (A) and receives a return pass into his running path (B).

- During the return pass, ② screens off ① on the inner side (C), who makes a step forward towards ③.

- ③ initially moves slightly to the left side and then immediately moves to the center (D).

- ③ must decide:
  - If ② remains defensive, ③ shoots from the back position (not shown in the figure).
  - If ② makes a step forward (E), ③ plays a pass into the gap (F), to ②, who leaves the screening position and eventually shoots at the goal (G).

- After the shot, ② and ② run to the other half of the court, and ④ starts the course on the other side (H).

⚠ The pivots should keep screening for as long as possible and leave the screening position as late as possible.

⚠ Switch offense players, defense players, and pivots after several rounds.

Handball Practice 14 – Interaction of back position players with the pivot – Shifting, Screening, and Using the Russian Screen

handball-uebungen.de
Trainingseinheiten und Übungen für Ihr Training!

No.: 1-7	Closing game	15	90

Setting:

- Define the playing field with a cone.

Course:

- Two teams play against each other 4-on-4.
- The attacking team plays 10 attacks, then the teams switch tasks.
- The teams get a point for each goal. If the goal is scored by the pivot or as a direct result of the pivot's screening actions (A, B, and C), the attacking team gets two points.
- Which team has scored highest after 10 attacks?

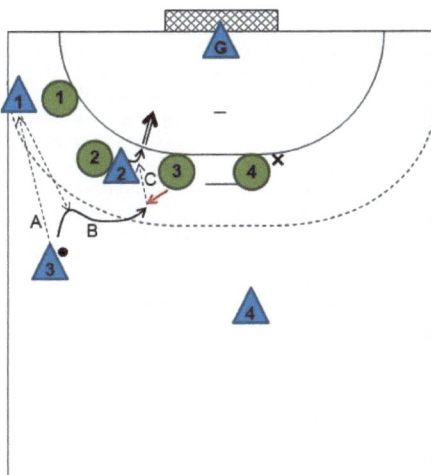

Notes:

_____

_____

_____

_____

_____

Handball Practice 14 – Interaction of back position players with the pivot – Shifting, Screening, and Using the Russian Screen

handball-uebungen.de
Trainingseinheiten und Übungen für Ihr Training!

TU 2:	Pivot – Achieving positional advantages in small-group team play	★ ★	90

Opening part		Main part				
X	Warm-up/Stretching	X	Offense/Individual		Jumping power	
	Running exercise	X	Offense/Small groups		Sprint contest	
X	Short game		Offense/Team		Goalkeeper	
	Coordination		Offense/Series of shots			
	Coordination run		Defense/Individual		**Final part**	
	Strengthening		Defense/Small groups	X	Closing game	
X	Ball familiarization		Defense/Team		Final sprint	
X	Goalkeeper warm-up shooting		Athletics			
			Endurance			

Key:

✖ Cone

▲1 Attacking player

●1 Defense player

⊡ Ball box

Equipment required:

Approx. 8-12 cones, ball box with sufficient number of handballs

Description:

The objective of this training unit is to improve the positioning of the pivot. Following warm-up and a short game, the players practice passing to the pivot under difficult conditions and with different passing variants during the ball familiarization and goalkeeper warm-up shooting phases. Afterwards, there will be an individual exercise regarding the pivot's screening followed by two small group exercises in which the interaction with the back position and wing players will be practiced. In a closing game, the players should implement what they practiced before.

The training unit consists of the following key exercises:
- Warm-up/Stretching (individual exercise: 10 minutes/total time: 10 minutes)
- Short game (10/20)
- Ball familiarization (15/35)
- Goalkeeper warm-up shooting (10/45)
- Offense/Individual (10/55)
- Offense/Small groups (10/65)
- Offense/Small groups (10/75)
- Closing game (15/90)

Training unit total time: 90 minutes

Handball Practice 14 – Interaction of back position players with the
pivot – Shifting, Screening, and Using the Russian Screen

handball-uebungen.de
Trainingseinheiten und Übungen für Ihr Training!

No.: 2-1	Warm-up/Stretching	10	10

Course:

- The players make pairs, with one ball per pair.
- The pairs crisscross through the 9-meter zone and continuously pass a ball.
- While doing this, the players try out different passing variants (bounce passes, passing over the head, passing behind the back).
- There is one team without a ball. The players of that team try to make the passing difficult for the other teams or even steal the ball. If they succeed, they start passing the stolen ball.

The players perform stretching exercises together.

No.: 2-2	Short game	10	20

Setting:

- Define two rectangular fields on two diagonal sides of the court with cones or with the lines on the gym floor.

Course:

- Make two teams. Both teams play team ball against each other.
- One player of each team stands inside of the previously defined rectangular fields.
- By playing quick passes (A) and moving in a well-coordinated manner, the team in ball possession tries to score points.
- The teams get a point when they manage to play a pass to their teammate inside of the rectangular field (B) and their teammate manages to play a return pass (C).
- The teams are allowed to score several times in a row; however, after they scored a point, the players must move to the other rectangular field where they may try to score the next point.
- The defending team tries to steal the ball and score points themselves.
- Who has scored highest when time is up?

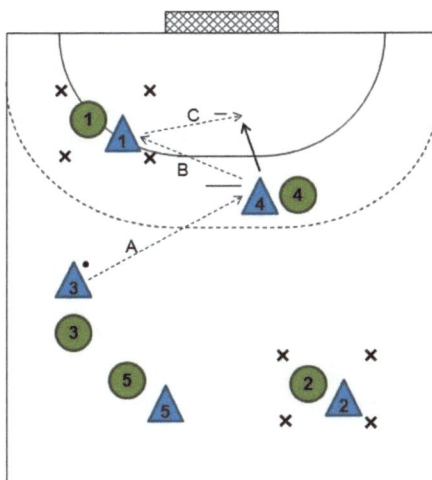

Variant:

- The players are allowed to play the return pass (C) to a random player of their team (and not necessarily to the player who played the initial pass).

Handball Practice 14 – Interaction of back position players with the pivot – Shifting, Screening, and Using the Russian Screen

handball-uebungen.de
Trainingseinheiten und Übungen für Ihr Training!

⚠ The players inside the rectangular fields must move cleverly in order to get the ball, and they should play the return pass at once.

⚠ The defense player inside the rectangular field should steal the ball, if possible. If he misses the ball, he should at least try to make the return passing as difficult as possible.

⚠ Regularly change the players in the rectangular fields.

No.: 2-3	Ball familiarization	15	35

Setting:
- Make teams of 5. Position two cones (with a distance of about 3-4 meters) per team.

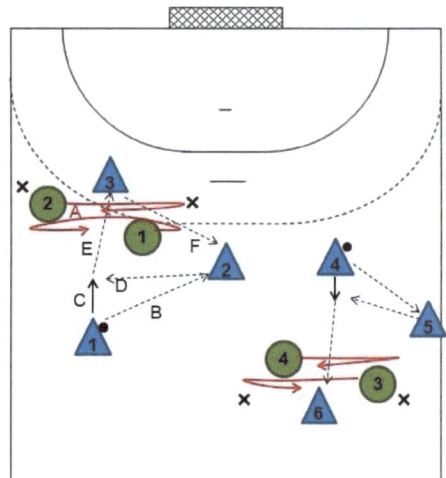

Course:
- Two players start as defense players (① and ②). They quickly sidestep between the cones in a slightly delayed manner. (A).
- ③ is the pivot and stands behind the two defense players.
- ① passes the ball to ② (B), initiates a piston movement (C), receives the ball from ② (D), and tries to pass to ③ (E).
- ③ plays a return pass to ② (F), and the course starts over.
- Other groups do the drill simultaneously. Switch the roles within the teams of 5 after several actions, until each player has played on each position.

Variant:
- ① should play a jump shot pass to ③ (E).

⚠ ① must keep an eye on the defense in order to get the right timing and to choose the right passing variant when passing the ball to ③.

⚠ The defense players keep sidestepping, may use their arms to block the ball, however.

Handball Practice 14 – Interaction of back position players with the pivot – Shifting, Screening, and Using the Russian Screen

handball-uebungen.de
Trainingseinheiten und Übungen für Ihr Training!

No.: 2-4	Goalkeeper warm-up shooting	10	45

Course:

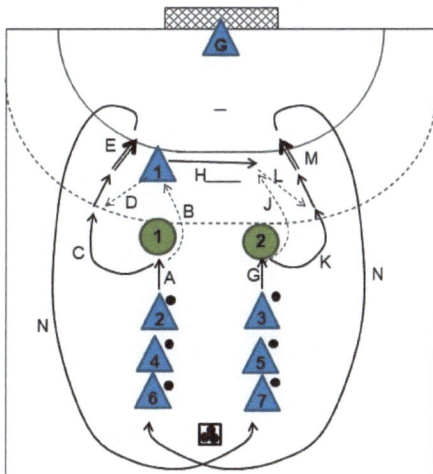

- **2** starts with a ball (A), passes around **1**'s body towards the 6-meter line, to **1** (B), moves back on the left side, starts over a piston movement (C), receives a return pass from **1** (D), and shoots at the left side of the goal as instructed (hands, top, bottom) (E).

- After **1** played the pass to **2** (D), **3** starts (G) and passes around **2**'s body (J), to **1**, who runs to the other side (H) and secures the ball.

- **3** moves back to the right side, starts another piston movement (K), receives the ball from **1** (L), and shoots at the right side of the goal as instructed (M).

- After the shot, the players line on the other side (N).

Passing variants (B and J):
- Feint a banana pass and "push" the ball through around the defense player's body.
- Feint "pushing through" the ball and play a banana pass.
- Pass through the defense player's legs.

Handball Practice 14 – Interaction of back position players with the pivot – Shifting, Screening, and Using the Russian Screen

handball-uebungen.de
Trainingseinheiten und Übungen für Ihr Training!

No.: 2-5	Offense/Individual	10	55

Course:

- ![1] passes to ![2] (A).
- ![2] passes to ![3] (B). While the pass is being played, ![1] moves into the defense next to ![1] (C) and tries to place a screen on the right side of the defense player.
- If ![1] manages to place the screen, ![3] passes to the pivot (D). ![1] takes positional advantage, secures the ball, and shoots at the goal.
- If ![1] moves along to the right side (E) and prevents ![1] from placing the screen, ![3] immediately plays a return pass to ![2] (F).
- ![1] quickly moves around ![1] and places a screen on the left side of ![1] (G).
- ![2] passes to the pivot (H), ![1] secures the ball, and shoots at the goal (J).
- Afterwards, ![4] starts the same course.

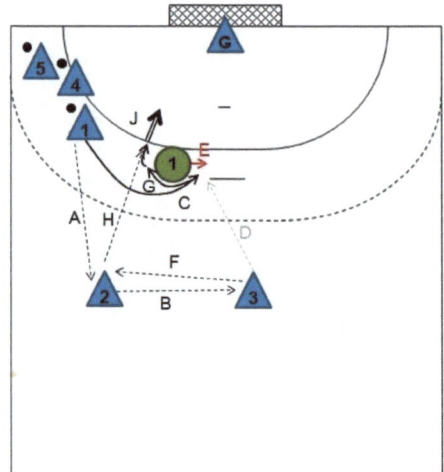

⚠ ![1] should clearly screen off ![1] and try to gain positional advantage for the second screen already during his first screening attempt.

Handball Practice 14 – Interaction of back position players with the pivot – Shifting, Screening, and Using the Russian Screen

handball-uebungen.de
Trainingseinheiten und Übungen für Ihr Training!

No.: 2-6	Offense/Small groups	10	65

Setting:
- Define the field size with two cones.

Course:
- The players initially pass a ball on the back positions.
- When 3 passes to 2 (B), 2 moves towards the wing position (A).
- Simultaneously, 1 places a screen next to 2.
- If 1 manages to gain positional advantage over 2, 2 plays a

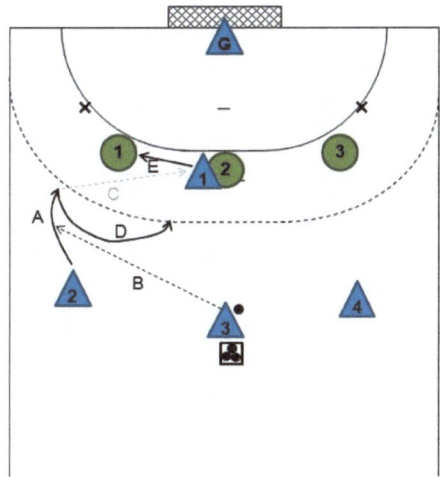

Figure 1

pass into the gap (C), to the pivot. 1 secures the ball and shoots at the goal.
- If 2 prevents the pass to 1 (C), 2 runs a curve towards the inner side (D).
- While the player above moves to the center, 1 places a screen next to 1 (E). If 1 makes a small step forward, 1 places the screen accordingly.
- 2 must decide now. If 2 remains defensive, 2 shoots (not shown in the figure).
- If 2 makes a small step forward (F), 2 passes to 1 (G) (jump shot pass, if applicable), who secures the ball and shoots at the goal (H).
- If 1 prevents the pass to 1, the players pass the ball to the other side (J and K), and 1 plays the same course on the other side with 4.
- Switch offense players, defense players, and the pivot (if applicable) after several rounds.

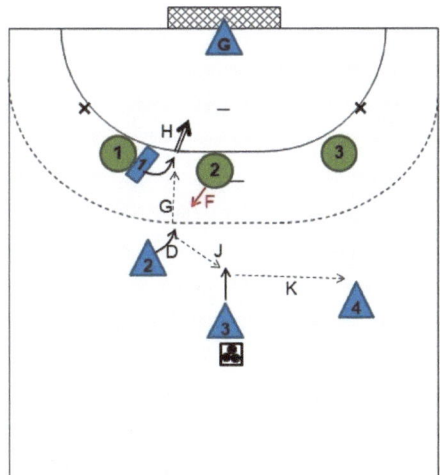

Figure 2

Handball Practice 14 – Interaction of back position players with the pivot – Shifting, Screening, and Using the Russian Screen

handball-uebungen.de
Trainingseinheiten und Übungen für Ihr Training!

⚠ 🔺**1** should screen clearly and try to gain positional advantage every time.

⚠ The back position players should clearly move towards the wing position and then powerfully move to the inner side in order to make room for the interaction with the pivot.

No.: 2-7	Offense/Small groups	10	75

Setting:
- Define the playing fields with cones on the left and right side.

Course:
- In this exercise, the wing player and the pivot play against two defense players.
- 🔺**4** passes to 🔺**2** (A).
- The wing player receives a pass (B) while standing on the outer wing position.
- While 🔺**2** plays the pass to 🔺**1** (B), the pivot (🔺**3**) places a screen on the outer side next to

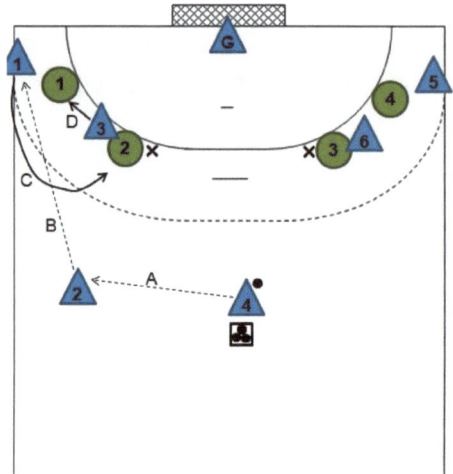

Figure 1

2 and may receive a direct pass from 🔺**1**, if **2** is inattentive (not shown in the figure).

- 🔺**1** starts moving towards the pass (B) and then runs a wide curve towards the center (C).
- While the player above moves to the center, 🔺**3** places a screen next to **1** (D).
- 🔺**1** must decide now. If **2** remains defensive, 🔺**1** shoots.

Handball Practice 14 – Interaction of back position players with the pivot – Shifting, Screening, and Using the Russian Screen

handball-uebungen.de
Trainingseinheiten und Übungen für Ihr Training!

- If (2) makes a step forward towards (1), the latter passes into the gap behind (2) (E), (3) secures the ball and shoots at the goal (F).
- (2) and (4) move to the other side after the action (G).
- (2) fetches a ball from the ball box and starts the course over on the right side.

⚠️ (3) should screen clearly and try to gain positional advantage every time.

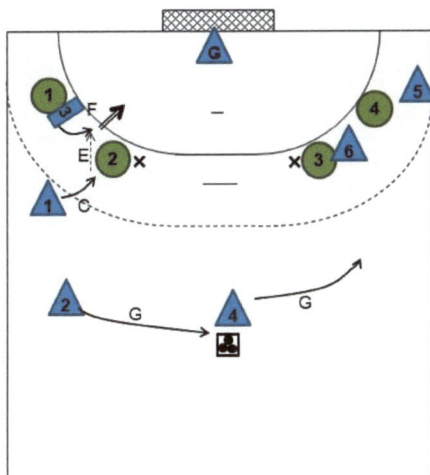

Figure 2

| No.: 2-8 | Closing game | 15 | 90 |

Setting:
- Divide the court in two halves with a cone.

Course:
- The attacking team initially plays 3-on-3 against a defending team ((1), (2), and (5) against (1), (2), and (3)) on the left side and has a feeder ((3)).
- The wing players and the back position players should try to interact with the pivot as practiced in the two previous exercises.
- For example, (2) initially moves towards the wing position after he received the pass from (3) (A) and then moves towards the center (B), (5) places a screen next to (2), receives the ball from (2) (C), and shoots at the goal (D).
- The attacking players get a point for each goal.
- After the action, the pivot ((5)) and a defense player (here: (3)) move to the other side (E).
- (2) becomes the new feeder (F) and (3) plays on the right back position (G).
- Afterwards, (3), (4), and (5) play against (3), (4), and (5).
- The defense and offense players switch tasks after 10 actions.
- Which team has shot the most goals?

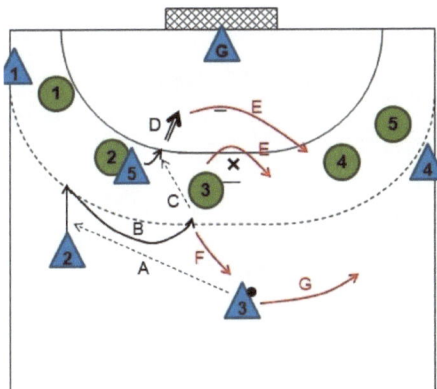

Handball Practice 14 – Interaction of back position players with the pivot – Shifting, Screening, and Using the Russian Screen

handball-uebungen.de
Trainingseinheiten und Übungen für Ihr Training!

TU 3:	Improving the interaction of back position players with the pivot	★★★	90

Opening part		Main part			
X	Warm-up/Stretching		Offense/Individual		Jumping power
	Running exercise	X	Offense/Small groups		Sprint contest
	Short game	X	Offense/Team		Goalkeeper
	Coordination		Offense/Series of shots		
X	Coordination run		Defense/Individual	**Final part**	
	Strengthening		Defense/Small groups		Closing game
X	Ball familiarization		Defense/Team		Final sprint
X	Goalkeeper warm-up shooting		Athletics		
			Endurance		

Key:

✖ Cone

△1 Attacking player

●1 Defense player

▣ Ball box

Equipment required:
➔ 1 "unball", 6 cones per team of 3, ball box with sufficient number of handballs

Description:

The objective of this training unit is to practice the interaction of a back position player with the pivot. Following warm-up and a running coordination exercise, the players prepare for the running moves in the back positions during the ball familiarization phase. After the goalkeeper warm-up shooting, there will be three offense exercises in which the players further develop the team play step by step. In a 4-on-4 game, the players should implement what they practiced before.

The training unit consists of the following key exercises:
- Warm-up/Stretching (individual exercise: 10 minutes/total time: 10 minutes)
- Coordination run (10/20)
- Ball familiarization (10/30)
- Goalkeeper warm-up shooting (10/40)
- Offense/Small groups (10/50)
- Offense/Small groups (10/60)
- Offense/Small groups (20/80)
- Offense/Team (10/90)

Training unit total time: 90 minutes

Handball Practice 14 – Interaction of back position players with the pivot – Shifting, Screening, and Using the Russian Screen

handball-uebungen.de
Trainingseinheiten und Übungen für Ihr Training!

No.: 3-1	Warm-up/Stretching	10	10

Setting:

-   The players are given sequential numbers.

Course:

-   The players crisscross through one half of the court and pass an "unball" (which is a ball that has its center of gravity displaced) in numerical order (1 to 2 to 3..., the last player passes to 1 etc.).
-   Add a handball after several rounds. The handball must be passed in reverse order (2 to 1 to the last player...) by playing bounce passes.
-   The players must do jumping jacks between the passes before they may receive the next pass.

⚠ The players should communicate to find out whether the player who is about to receive a pass is ready or must do the jumping jack movement first.

Handball Practice 14 – Interaction of back position players with the
pivot – Shifting, Screening, and Using the Russian Screen

handball-uebungen.de
Trainingseinheiten und Übungen für Ihr Training!

No.: 3-2	Coordination run	10	20

Setting:
- The players make groups of 3 and stand near the side line as shown in the figure.
- Each group of 3 positions six cones in the center as shown in the figure.

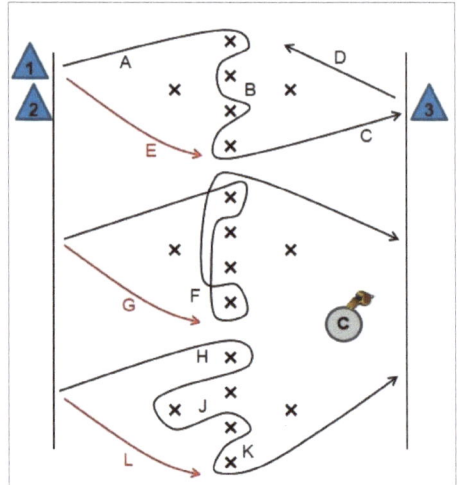

Course 1:
- On command, one player of each team (1) starts to sprint (A), sidesteps around the four cones in slalom (B) from left to right, sprints to the other side (C), and exchanges a high five with his teammate (3) there.
- 3 starts the same course (D) and exchanges a high five on the other side with 2 etc.
- The players repeat the course until c whistles after a minute. This is the sign for the players to switch the course for another minute, i.e. the players start to sprint from the other side and do the sidestep from right to left (E).
- The players may take a short break after the two minutes.

Afterwards, course 2 starts:
- The players run around the cones as shown in the figure. They may choose the running direction (forward, backward, sidestep) themselves (F).
- c whistles again after a minute. This is the sign for the players to run towards the cones from the other side (G).
- The players may take a short break after the two minutes.

Afterwards, course 3 starts:
- The players run around the cones as shown in the figure.
- They run around the first three cones by doing quick forward and backward movements (H and J).
- The players run around the last cone sidestepping (K).
- c whistles again after a minute. This is the sign for the players to run towards the cones from the other side (L).

Handball Practice 14 – Interaction of back position players with the pivot – Shifting, Screening, and Using the Russian Screen

handball-uebungen.de
Trainingseinheiten und Übungen für Ihr Training!

No.: 3-3	Ball familiarization	10	30

Setting:

- Position 8 cones as shown in the figure.

Course 1:

- ▲1 makes a dynamic piston movement forward (A) and passes the ball into the piston movement path of ▲3 (B).
- After the pass (A), ▲1 immediately moves back and lines up behind ▲5 again (C).
- ▲3 also makes a dynamic piston movement forward and passes the ball to ▲5 (D) etc.
- ▲4 starts simultaneously with ▲1 and makes the same movements (E).

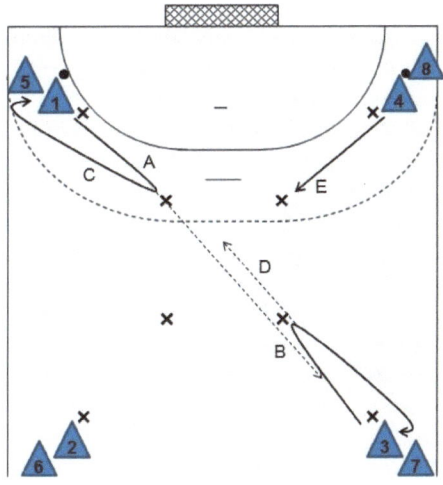

Course 2:

- ▲2 runs forward dynamically while ▲1 passes the ball into his running path (F).
- ▲2 makes a running feint to the left side of the cone while holding the ball (he must not bounce it), feints a stem shot (G), dribbles dynamically around the cone, makes a piston movement forward (H), and eventually passes the ball into the piston movement path of ▲3 (J).
- ▲3 repeats the movements and passes to ▲4 (K).
- And so on.

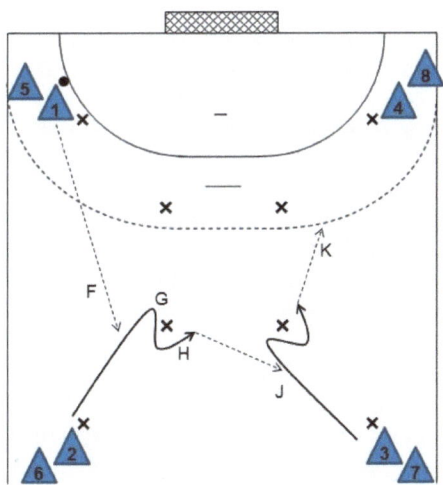

⚠ The piston movement (A and B) towards the cone must be carried out dynamically; the pass (B and D) should be initiated with a stem shot feint.

Handball Practice 14 – Interaction of back position players with the pivot – Shifting, Screening, and Using the Russian Screen

handball-uebungen.de
Trainingseinheiten und Übungen für Ihr Training!

No.: 3-4	Goalkeeper warm-up shooting	10	40

Setting:

- Two players each line up between the 6- and 9-meter lines.
- The players in the back each hold a ball.
- The players in the front (without ball) stand with their legs spread and their faces turned towards the goal.

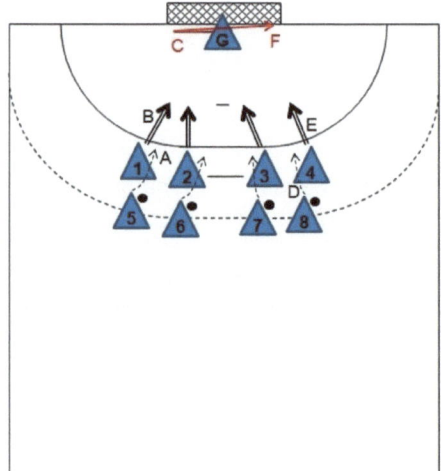

Course:

- **5** dribbles his ball forward through the legs of **1** (A) in such a way that **1** can pick it up after it touched the ground and shoot at the goal (B).

- **1** shoots as instructed (top, middle, bottom) at the left side of the goal so that **G** is able to save the shot from the center of the goal (C).

- While **1** shoots, **8** dribbles his ball through the legs of **4** (D). **4** picks up the ball and shoots at the right side of the goal as instructed (top, middle, bottom).

- After the first shot (B), **G** immediately moves to the other side of the goal and tries (F) to save the ball thrown by **4** (E).

- Repeat the course with shoots of the players **2** and **3**.

- Afterwards, the teams switch tasks.

⚠ The players should shoot the series of 4 shots in such a way that there is a smooth flow for **G**. Adjust the timing to the speed of **G** when dribbling through the legs.

Handball Practice 14 – Interaction of back position players with the pivot – Shifting, Screening, and Using the Russian Screen

handball-uebungen.de
Trainingseinheiten und Übungen für Ihr Training!

No.: 3-5	Offense/Small groups	10	50

Setting:

- Define two small playing fields with cones as shown in the figure.
- In each corridor of cones there is a defense player and a pivot.

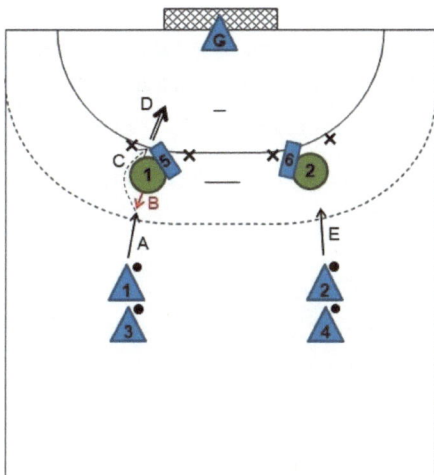

Course:

- ▲1 dribbles a ball straight forward towards ①1 (A).

- ①1 steps forward towards the movement path of ▲1 (B).

- ▲5 keeps his position behind ①1 and stays at the 6-meter line.

- ▲1 passes to ▲5, around ①1's body (C).

- ▲5 shoots at the goal (D).

- Repeat the course on the other side (E). And so on.

⚠ ▲1 tries different passing variants when passing to ▲5 (passing through the legs, over the head of ①1, around the body on the right/left side, with a feint).

⚠ ①1 should clearly step forward towards the movement path of ▲1 and try to prevent the pass using his arms; he should not attack ①1 directly, however. A pass should be possible.

No.: 3-6	Offense/Small groups	10	60

Setting:

- At the beginning of the exercise, define a wide corridor of cones.
- 6 stands between 1 and 2.
- 7 waits at the side until it is his turn.

Course:

- 1 dribbles a ball slightly to the left of 1 (A).
- 1 makes a step forward towards the movement path of 1 and moves along with him (B).
- 6 places a screen next to 2 (C).
- 1 passes the ball to 6 in direction of the 6-meter line (D).
- 6 takes up the ball and shoots at the goal (E).
- After the pass, 1 immediately sprints to the center line, fetches a new ball and lines up again (F).
- Afterwards, repeat the course with 2. 2 dribbles to the other side, towards the right of 2, and 6 places a screen next to 1.
- After these two actions, 7 makes two actions etc.
- Narrow the corridor of cones after several courses to make the space for passing the ball to 6 (7) smaller.

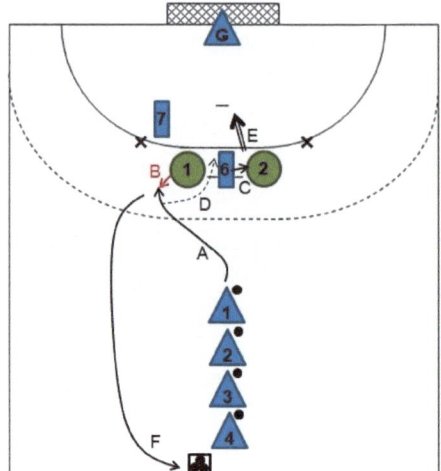

⚠ 1 must come to 1 as close as possible so that 1 is forced to make a step forward. However, he must not come too close to 1 since otherwise he will be body blocked.

⚠ 1 should make a step forward towards the movement path of 1 and try to block the pass with his arms. If 1 comes too close, 1 may also try to body block (throwing hand).

Handball Practice 14 – Interaction of back position players with the pivot – Shifting, Screening, and Using the Russian Screen

handball-uebungen.de
Trainingseinheiten und Übungen für Ihr Training!

No.: 3-7	Offense/Small groups		20	80

Setting:

- Define a corridor of cones as in the previous exercise.

Course:

- ▲1 passes the ball to ▲2 and receives a return pass into his movement to the left (A).

- ⬣6 should place a screen next to ⚫2, diagonally to the running path (B).

- ▲1 dynamically dribbles the ball to the right side and forces ⚫2 to move along with him (C).

- ⬣6 moves next to ⚫1 and places a screen (D) as soon as ▲1 starts to move diagonally.

- ⚫2 makes a step forward towards ▲1 (E).

- ▲1 passes the ball around ⚫2's body, to ⬣6, who still screens off ⚫1 (F).

- ⬣6 shoots at the goal (G).

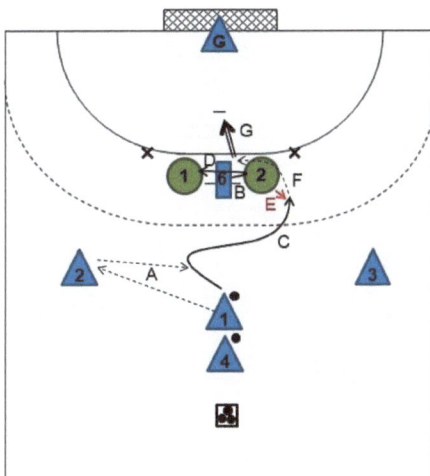

⚠ ▲1 and ⬣6 must get into visual contact during the action.

⚠ ⬣6 must place the screen in such a way that the screened defense player is unable to move around and block the pass.

⚠ ⬣6 may use his body only for screening (legs apart), he is not allowed to use his hands.

Handball Practice 14 – Interaction of back position players with the pivot – Shifting, Screening, and Using the Russian Screen

handball-uebungen.de
Trainingseinheiten und Übungen für Ihr Training!

Extension:

- ▲1 may chose his running path towards the defense freely; he may move towards the defense directly or force the defense players to move along with him.
- ▲6 should react to the running movement of ▲1 and place the screen accordingly.
- ▲1 may now also try to break through if the defense players do not step forward towards ▲1 courageously enough (H).

Competition:

- ▲1 and ▲6 play five attacks against ●1 and ●2; afterwards, they switch roles. Which team has shot the most goals?
- ▲2 and ▲3 serve as receivers during the team play.
- Afterwards, repeat the course with four new players.

No.: 3-8	Offense/Team		10	90

Setting:

- Two teams play against each other 4-on-4.

Course:

- The attacking team tries to get in a good shooting position by implementing the interaction with ▲6 which they practiced before. If the attacking players succeed and the pivot scores a goal, they get two points.
- However, the attacking players may also try to break through if the defense players do not step forward towards the piston movement courageously but rather try to prevent the pass to the pivot. If the attacking players succeed in doing this and score a goal, they get one point.
- Which team has scored highest after five (10) attacks?

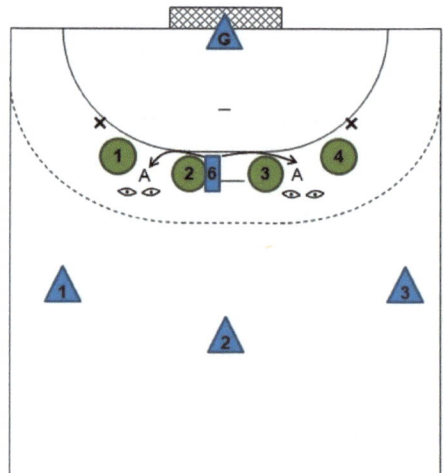

⚠ The attacking players communicate with ▲6 through visual contact so that he is able to position himself between two defense players accordingly (A).

Handball Practice 14 – Interaction of back position players with the pivot – Shifting, Screening, and Using the Russian Screen

handball-uebungen.de
Trainingseinheiten und Übungen für Ihr Training!

TU 4:	Small group game: Piston movement/countermovement of the back position players and interaction with the pivot	★★★	90

Opening part		Main part			
X	Warm-up/Stretching	X	Offense/Individual		Jumping power
	Running exercise	X	Offense/Small groups		Sprint contest
	Short game	X	Offense/Team		Goalkeeper
	Coordination		Offense/Series of shots		
	Coordination run		Defense/Individual		**Final part**
	Strengthening		Defense/Small groups		Closing game
X	Ball familiarization		Defense/Team		Final sprint
X	Goalkeeper warm-up shooting		Athletics		
			Endurance		

Key:

✖ Cone

△1 Attacking player

●1 Defense player

⊞ Ball box

Equipment required:
→ 8 cones, ball box with sufficient number of handballs

Description:

This training unit focuses on the interaction of the back position players with each other regarding piston movement/countermovement and passing to the pivot. Following warm-up, the back position players take the first methodical step regarding the interaction with the pivot during the ball familiarization phase. During the goalkeeper warm-up shooting and a subsequent offense exercise, the players practice the piston movement/countermovement which should result in a shot. In the following two small group exercises, the players stepwise further develop their piston movement/countermovement and the interaction with the pivot. The final exercise combines the different elements that the players practiced before with an initial action and creative continuous playing.

The training unit consists of the following key exercises:
- Warm-up/Stretching (individual exercise: 10 minutes/total time: 10 minutes)
- Warm-up/Stretching (10/20)
- Ball familiarization (10/30)
- Goalkeeper warm-up shooting (10/40)
- Offense/Individual (10/50)
- Offense/Small groups (15/65)
- Offense/Small groups (15/80)
- Offense/Team (10/90)

Training unit total time: 90 minutes

Handball Practice 14 – Interaction of back position players with the pivot – Shifting, Screening, and Using the Russian Screen

handball-uebungen.de
Trainingseinheiten und Übungen für Ihr Training!

No.: 4-1	Warm-up/Stretching	10	10

Course:

- The players move independently through the court dribbling a ball while making different running moves (forward, backward, sidestep).
- Two players get into visual contact, dribble towards each other and pass their balls, make a running feint in front of each other (both to the same side!) and do an easy jump, i.e. either left-right-jump or right-left-jump. Afterwards, they keep on jogging and look for another teammate for the next action.

The players perform stretching exercises together.

No.: 4-2	Warm-up/Stretching	10	20

Setting:

- Divide the 6- to 9-meter zone into five sections (see figure), depending on the number of players.
- There are three players and one ball in each section.

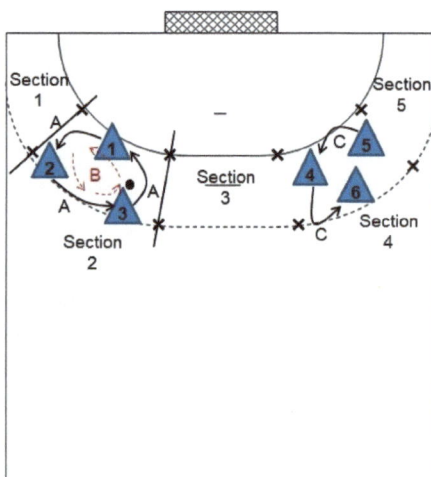

Course:

- The three players move freely within their section of the playing field (A) and roll the ball on the floor using their hands (B).

Variants while moving inside of the playing field:

- Rolling the ball in running direction and against the running direction to the next player.
- The players do the following tasks between the rolling movements:
  - Forward/backward arm rotation.
  - Do 1 jumping jack.
  - Once the players have rolled the ball to the next player, they must touch the 6- or 9-meter line with their hand (C).
  - Pass the ball with the foot.

Handball Practice 14 – Interaction of back position players with the
pivot – Shifting, Screening, and Using the Russian Screen

handball-uebungen.de
Trainingseinheiten und Übungen für Ihr Training!

No.: 4-3	Ball familiarization	10	30

Setting:

- Divide the 6- to 9-meter zone into five sections (see figure).
- There are three players and one ball in each section.

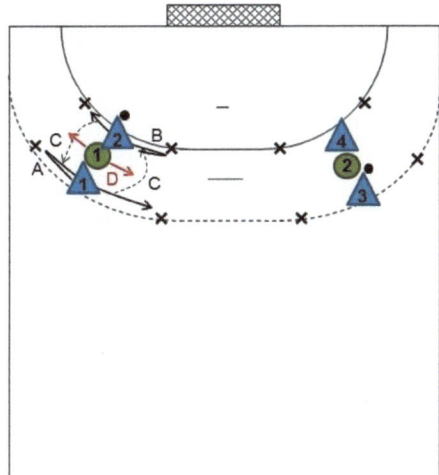

Course:

- 1 and 2 move between the two cones on the 9-meter line (A) and the 6-meter line (B).

- 1 and 2 pass a ball around 1's body while moving (C). In the beginning, the players should not play bounce passes but direct passes.

- 1 should keep turning towards the player holding the ball so that he can see him and then try to block the pass sidestepping (D).

Variant:

- Allow bounce passes.

⚠️ 1 and 2 should move within the zone between the 6- and 9-meter line, not beyond.

⚠️ 2 must be careful not to step into the 6-meter zone.

Handball Practice 14 – Interaction of back position players with the pivot – Shifting, Screening, and Using the Russian Screen

handball-uebungen.de
Trainingseinheiten und Übungen für Ihr Training!

No.: 4-4	Goalkeeper warm-up shooting	10	40

Setting:

- Position six cones as shown in the figure.
- Provide a ball box.

Course:

- **1** starts dynamically and receives a pass from **7** into his running path (A).

- At the cone, **1** feints a stem shot at the goal (B).

- **1** dribbles around the cone that is positioned a bit closer to the goal (C), runs dynamically towards the goal after the last cone, and eventually shoots at the left side of the goal as instructed (top, middle, bottom) (D).

- Immediately after the initial action of **1** (B and C), the course starts over on the other side with **4** and **8** shooting at the right side of the goal as instructed (top, middle, bottom) (E) in order to provide **G** with a series of shots.

- As soon as each player has done the course, **7** and **8** eventually shoot at the goal after each other, whereas **7** shoots at the left side and **8** shoots at the right side of the goal (F).

- Change **7** and **8** in the next round.

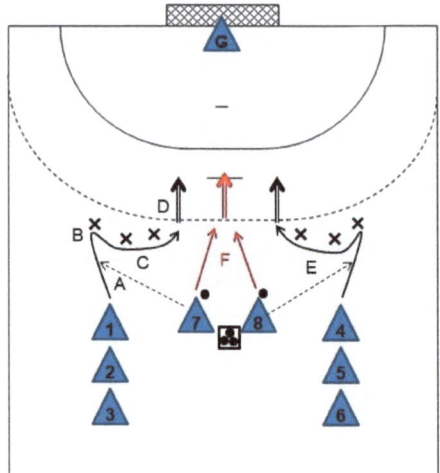

⚠️ **1** must receive the pass from **7** in such a way (A) that he is able to shoot at once, without dribbling (B).

Handball Practice 14 – Interaction of back position players with the pivot – Shifting, Screening, and Using the Russian Screen

handball-uebungen.de
Trainingsainheiten und Übungen für Ihr Training!

No.: 4-5	Offense/Individual	10	50

Setting:

- Provide a ball box with a sufficient number of handballs

Course:

- 1 starts dynamically and receives a pass from 7 into his running path (A).

- On the left side, next to 1, 1 feints a stem shot at the goal (B).

- 1 dribbles around 1 (C), runs dynamically towards the goal and eventually shoots at the goal (D).

- 1 should clearly step forward towards 1 (E) and move along with him but allow the movement (F).

(Figure 1)

- Repeat the course on the other side (G). And so on.
- The attacking players change sides after each action.
- Substitute 7, 8, 1, and 2 regularly.

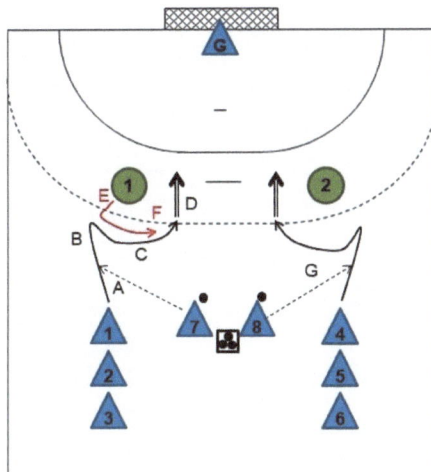

⚠ 1 must make a clear piston movement to the left and feint a stem shot so that 1 is forced to react.

⚠ 1 must dribble around 1 (C) in such a way that his own body is between the ball and 1, i.e. dribble with the right hand to prevent 1 from stealing the ball.

⚠ If 1 is left-handed, he takes the ball into his right hand after feinting the stem shot (B), dribbles around 1, and takes the ball into his left hand again for the shot. Same course for right-handed players on the other side, also with changing hands.

Handball Practice 14 – Interaction of back position players with the pivot – Shifting, Screening, and Using the Russian Screen

handball-uebungen.de
Trainingseinheiten und Übungen für Ihr Training!

Extension (① should act variably now):

- If ① does not step forward towards the lateral running path of ▲① courageously enough (H), ▲① breaks through on the left side (J) and eventually shoots at the goal (K).

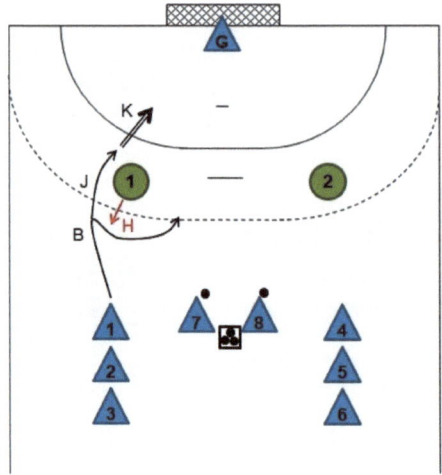

(Figure 2)

Handball Practice 14 – Interaction of back position players with the pivot – Shifting, Screening, and Using the Russian Screen

handball-uebungen.de
Trainingseinheiten und Übungen für Ihr Training!

No.: 4-6	Offense/Small groups	15	65

Setting:

- Define the playing field with 8 cones as shown in the figure.

Course:

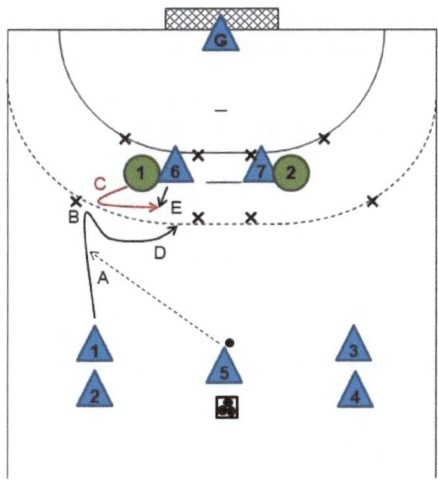

- ▲1 dynamically runs towards the cone and receives a pass from ▲5 into his path (A).

- As soon as he is in line with the cone, ▲1 feints a stem shot (plants left foot firmly on the ground and feints a shot) (B).

- ●1 should move towards ▲1's piston movement (C).

(Figure 1)

- ▲1 dribbles around ●1 dynamically; ▲1 must force his defensive counterpart to move along with him (D)!

- ▲6 steps forward and screens off ●1 so that he cannot move any further (C and E).

- ▲6 leaves his screening position next to ●1, moves back towards the 6-meter line (F), and receives a pass from ▲1 directed at the goal zone (G).

- ▲6 shoots at the goal (H).

- Afterwards, repeat the drill on the other side (J).

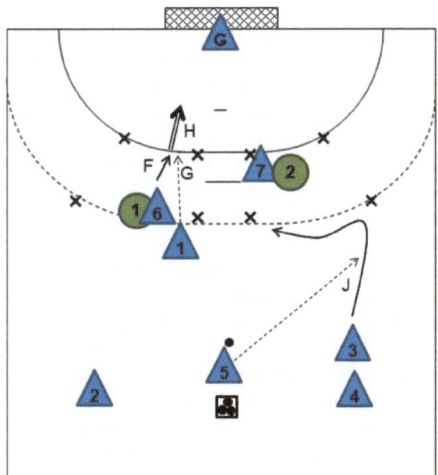

⚠ ▲1 must not dribble the ball before he feints the stem shot (B)!

⚠ ▲6 may screen off ●1 with his body only (E), he must not use his arms (offensive foul).

(Figure 2)

⚠ ▲6 should not receive a direct pass, but rather a bounce pass towards the 6-meter line (G) so that ▲6 can pick up the ball while moving and can shoot immediately.

Handball Practice 14 – Interaction of back position players with the pivot – Shifting, Screening, and Using the Russian Screen

handball-uebungen.de
Trainingseinheiten und Übungen für Ihr Training!

No.: 4-7	Offense/Small groups	15	80

Setting:

- Position six cones for the playing corridors as shown in the figure.

Course:

- **6** places a screen next to **2**.

- **1** starts dynamically and receives a pass from **5** into his running path (A).

- On the left side, next to **1**, **1** feints a stem shot at the goal (B).

- **1** should clearly move towards **1** (C).

(Figure 1)

- **1** dribbles around **1** and dynamically approaches the goal (D).

- **6** leaves his position next to **2** and places a screen on the inner side of **1**'s running path (E):

  o If **2** remains defensive, **1** makes a jump shot at the goal (F).

  o If **2** actively steps forward (H) to block **1**'s shot (F), **1** plays a bounce pass around **2** towards the goal zone (J). **6** leaves his screening position next to **1** (E), moves back towards the 6-meter line and towards the ball (K), picks up the ball, and shoots at the goal (L).

- Repeat the course on the other side, whereas **2** changes the side (G) – now making up the defense together with **3**.

(Figure 2)

Handball Practice 14 – Interaction of back position players with the pivot – Shifting, Screening, and Using the Russian Screen

handball-uebungen.de
Trainingseinheiten und Übungen für Ihr Training!

⚠️ If 1️⃣ does not offensively move towards 🔺's path (C), 🔺 may also break through on the left side of 1️⃣ or make a jump shot from the 9-meter line.

⚠️ 🔺6 must not use his hands in order to screen off his counterpart sideways (E) (offensive foul). Preferably, he should cross his arms over his chest or hold his hands in catching position.

⚠️ The pass to 🔺6 must not be played in direction of 🔺6's screening position (E), but rather into the gap in direction of the goal zone (J).

Handball Practice 14 – Interaction of back position players with the pivot – Shifting, Screening, and Using the Russian Screen

handball-uebungen.de
Trainingseinheiten und Übungen für Ihr Training!

No.: 4-8	Offense/Team	10	90

Setting:

- Define the playing field with two cones as shown in the figure.

Course:

- 1 receives a pass from 2 into his running path (A).

- 6 initially stands next to 2.

- 1 dynamically moves to the other back position and crosses 3 (B) who runs towards the goal with the ball.

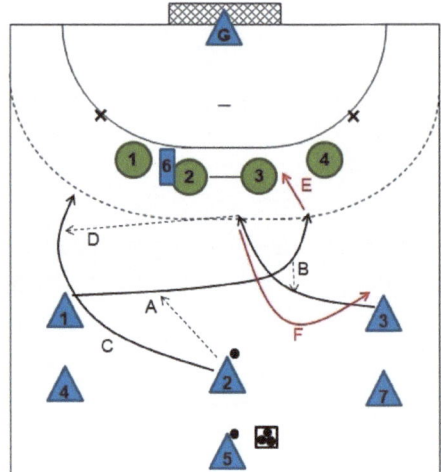

- After the initial pass, 2 runs a curve towards the back position (C) and receives a pass from 3 into his running path (D).

- 1 moves towards the 6-meter zone next to 3 (E).

- 3 moves back to his back position at once after the crossing (F).

- 2 feints a stem shot on the left side next to 1 who is stepping forward, and dynamically dribbles around 1 (G).

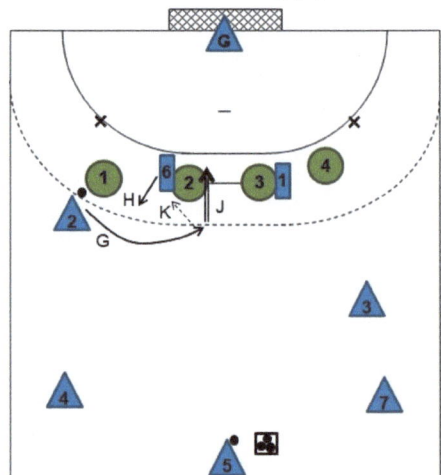

- 6 should block 1's defense movements by placing a screen next to him (H):

  o If 2 remains defensive, 2 makes a jump shot at the goal (J).

  o If 2 makes a step forward, 2 plays a bounce pass in direction of the goal zone to 6 who is leaving his screening position (K).

(Figure 1)

(Figure 2)

Handball Practice 14 – Interaction of back position players with the pivot – Shifting, Screening, and Using the Russian Screen

handball-uebungen.de
Trainingseinheiten und Übungen für Ihr Training!

- If the defense players block both options (J and K), ▲2 passes the ball to ▲3 into his dynamic running movement (L).
- ▲2 moves back to his back position (O) immediately after he played the pass (L).
- ▲3 feints a stem shot on the right side next to ●4 who is stepping forward, and dynamically dribbles around ●4 (M).
- ▲1 leaves ●3 and places a screen next to ●4 (N).
- ▲3 may now shoot himself, interact with ▲1 on the pivot position, or pass the ball back to ▲2 (P).
- Repeat the course until the defending players are no longer able to move along with the attacking players and the attacking players succeed and manage to shoot at the goal.

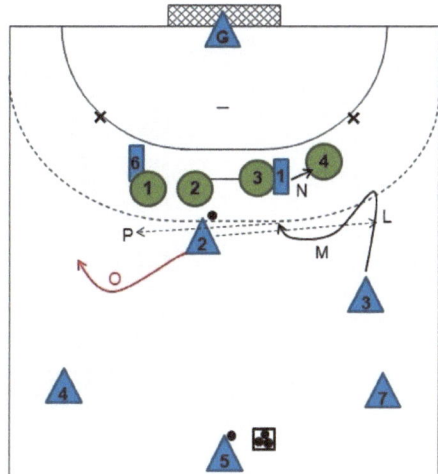

⚠ The actions of each individual attacking player must be threatening enough to force a reaction of the defending players.

⚠ If the defending players do not react actively to an attacking player's action, the attacking player may try to shoot at the goal anytime.

⚠ After they played the pass, ▲2 and ▲3 must move back to their initial positions (F and O) to be able to start a subsequent action.

Notes:

_____

_____

_____

_____

Handball Practice 14 – Interaction of back position players with the pivot – Shifting, Screening, and Using the Russian Screen

handball-uebungen.de
Trainingseinheiten und Übungen für Ihr Training!

TU 5:	Acting against the defending wing position player with a physically stronger pivot	★★★★	90

Opening part		Main part				
X	Warm-up/Stretching	X	Offense/Individual		Jumping power	
	Running exercise	X	Offense/Small groups		Sprint contest	
	Short game	X	Offense/Team		Goalkeeper	
	Coordination		Offense/Series of shots		**Final part**	
X	Coordination run		Defense/Individual			
	Strengthening		Defense/Small groups	X	Closing game	
X	Ball familiarization		Defense/Team		Final sprint	
X	Goalkeeper warm-up shooting		Athletics			
			Endurance			

Key:

✗ Cone

△1 Attacking player

○1 Defense player

▭ Large safety mat

▣ Ball box

▭ Coordination ladder

Equipment required:
➔ 1 coordination ladder
6 cones per team of three, ball box with sufficient number of handballs, whistle

Description:

This training unit focuses on simple initial actions in order to gain positional advantage by having a physically stronger pivot play against a physically weaker defense player on the wing positions. The warm-up phase focuses on coordination. Afterwards, the players practice the first steps of the subsequent team play during the ball familiarization and goalkeeper warm-up shooting phases. The three subsequent offense exercises consist of the preparation and the final 1-on-1 play to get the pivot into a good shooting position. A closing game completes this training unit.

The training unit consists of the following key exercises:
- Warm-up/Stretching (individual exercise: 10 minutes/total time: 10 minutes)
- Coordination run (10/20)
- Ball familiarization (10/30)
- Goalkeeper warm-up shooting (10/40)
- Offense/Individual (10/50)
- Offense/Small groups (15/65)
- Offense/Team (15/80)
- Closing game (10/90)

Training unit total time: 90 minutes

Handball Practice 14 – Interaction of back position players with the pivot – Shifting, Screening, and Using the Russian Screen

handball-uebungen.de
Trainingseinheiten und Übungen für Ihr Training!

No.: 5-1	Warm-up/Stretching	10	10

Setting:
- Position four cones as shown in the figure.

Course:
- The players initially jog around the cones in a circle and do the following tasks each over a few rounds:
  - o Easy jogging
  - o Hopping
  - o Sidestepping
- After a few rounds, the players at the center line and at the 6-meter line (A) start doing the following jump variants alternately:
  - o Three jumps with the right leg (B), three jumps with the left leg (C) etc., whereas they must always jump over the line.
  - o Jump with the right leg, jump with the left leg, jump and land on both feet (D). The players must always jump over the line. Repeat the course; however, the players always must start with the right leg (E) and so on.

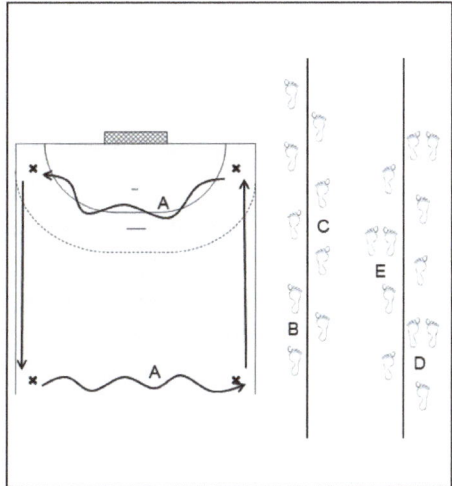

The players perform stretching exercises together.

Handball Practice 14 – Interaction of back position players with the pivot – Shifting, Screening, and Using the Russian Screen

handball-uebungen.de
Trainingseinheiten und Übungen für Ihr Training!

No.: 5-2	Coordination run	10	20

Setting:
- Put the coordination ladder on the floor.

Course 1:
- The players jump through the coordination ladder as follows:
  - Land with both feet in the interspace
  - Jump out of the ladder and land with feet to the left and right of the ladder (A)
- At the end, the players jog back easily and line up again for the next round.

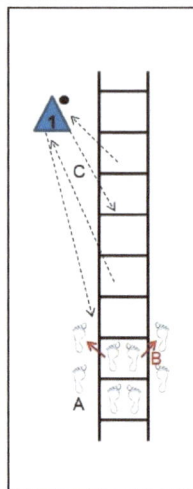

Course 2:
- The jumping course remains the same as in course 1.
- Now there will be a change of the jumping rhythm, however:
  - The players jump into the ladder (land with both feet) at normal (slow) speed
  - When jumping out, the players speed up considerably (B) so that the speed changes continuously along the way

Course 3:
- The course remains the same as in course 2, but the rhythm is switched now:
  - When jumping into the ladder, the players must speed up considerably.
  - The players jump out of the ladder at normal (slow) speed

Course 4:
- Repeat course 1 to 3. The player who runs through the coordination ladder, plays 2 passes with (C and figures below).
- The player in the coordination ladder should do the jumping course simultaneously.

Overall course:
- Each player must do the exercise 4 times.

⚠️ The players should have their head up and view forward. They should not look at their feet.

Handball Practice 14 – Interaction of back position players with the pivot – Shifting, Screening, and Using the Russian Screen

handball-uebungen.de
Trainingseinheiten und Übungen für Ihr Training!

No.: 5-3	Ball familiarization	10	30

Setting:

- Make groups of 3 and position six cones as shown in the figure.

Basic setting:

- 1 runs around the cones in a circle and passes a ball.

Course:

- 1 passes the ball to 3 (A) and receives a return pass when passing the cone (B).

- 1 runs around the cone, passes 2 the ball (C) and receives a return pass when passing the cone (D).

- Afterwards, 1 runs around the cone and passes the ball to 3 (A).

- And so on.

- After the pass (B and D), 3 and 2 immediately start to sidestep dynamically around the cones on the "8 path" (E). The players' viewing direction is towards the center (F).

Switch the players after a few rounds.

Handball Practice 14 – Interaction of back position players with the
pivot – Shifting, Screening, and Using the Russian Screen

handball-uebungen.de
Trainingseinheiten und Übungen für Ihr Training!

No.: 5-4	Goalkeeper warm-up shooting	10	40

Setting:

- Position two cones for the body feint as shown in the figure.

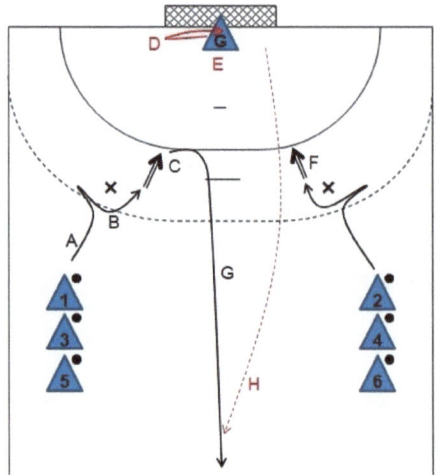

Course:

- 1 starts the drill and dribbles towards the cone (A).

- 1 picks up the ball in front of the cone, makes an extensive body feint to the left, runs around the cone on the right side and towards the goal (B), and shoots at the left side of the goal as instructed (top, middle, bottom).

- G starts from the center of the goal, tries to save the ball shot to the left side of the goal (D), and then immediately moves back to the center of the goal (E).

- As soon as 1 runs towards the goal, 2 starts the same course and shoots at the right side of the goal (F).

⚠ G should start his movement from the center of the goal and not stand in the respective corner already.

- The players immediately sprint to the center line after the shot (G).

- The last shooting player receives a pass from G towards the center line (H) (for a fast throw-off).

⚠ The players must coordinate their movements in order to provide G with a series of shots.

Handball Practice 14 – Interaction of back position players with the pivot – Shifting, Screening, and Using the Russian Screen

handball-uebungen.de
Trainingseinheiten und Übungen für Ihr Training!

No.: 5-5	Offense/Individual		10	50

Setting:

- Position two cones as shooting point as shown in the figure.

Course:

- 1 and 2 stand in the middle between the 6- and 9-meter lines.

- 1 starts the course by bouncing the ball once (A). This is the starting sign for 1 and 2.

- 1 tries to run around 2 in the zone between the 6- and 9-meter lines (B) in order to block the pass from 1 to 2. He must not change his initially chosen running direction (either running behind or in front of 2) (F).

- 2 screens off 1 for approx. two seconds (C). Then c whistles (D). 2 immediately leaves the screening position, picks up the ball 1 passed towards the 6-meter line, and eventually shoots at the goal (E).

- Repeat the course on the other side with bouncing the ball as the starting sign (G).

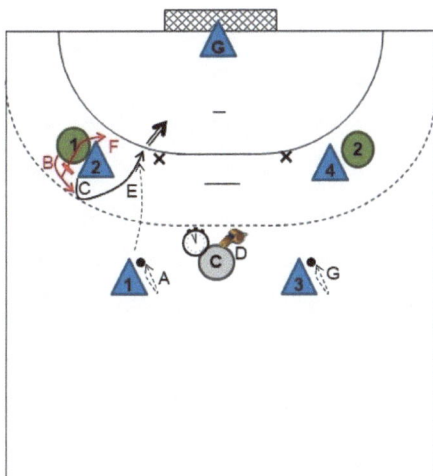

⚠ In the beginning of the exercise, the defending players should defend with an intensity of approx. 50-60%. During the further course of the exercise, the defending players should increase the pressure and try to block the passes.

⚠ 2 may use his body only for screening off 1. He must not use his hands and should hold them in front of his body instead.

Handball Practice 14 – Interaction of back position players with the pivot – Shifting, Screening, and Using the Russian Screen

handball-uebungen.de
Trainingseinheiten und Übungen für Ihr Training!

No.: 5-6	Offense/Small groups	15	65

Setting:

- Position two cones as shown in the figure.
- Provide a ball box with a sufficient number of handballs

Course:

- ▲3 stands between ①and ② in the beginning.

- ▲2 starts the course and receives a pass from ▲1 into his running path (A).

- ② steps forward actively into the movement path (B).

- ▲2 moves towards the center and plays 1-on-1 against ② (C).

- As soon as ② moves along with ▲2 towards the center (D), ▲3 places a screen next to ① (E) so that ① cannot move around ▲3 in order to block the subsequent pass (F).

⚠ ▲3 must not use his hands for the screening. He should place the screen using his body only.

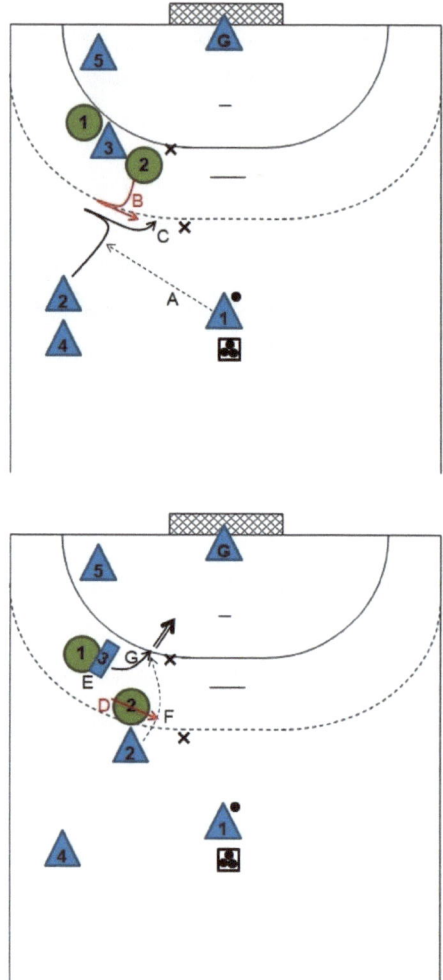

- ▲2 plays a bounce pass in direction of the goal zone (F), ▲3 leaves ① towards the goal zone, picks up the ball, and eventually shoots at the goal (G).
- Afterwards, repeat the course on the right side (not shown in the figure).

⚠ The pass (F) must be played in direction of the goal zone, i.e. not in direction of ▲3 's position. ▲3 should run towards the ball and pick it up. If the players do well, ▲2 may play a long pass in direction of the goal zone.

Handball Practice 14 – Interaction of back position players with the pivot – Shifting, Screening, and Using the Russian Screen

handball-uebungen.de
Trainingseinheiten und Übungen für Ihr Training!

No.: 5-7	Offense/Team	15	80

Setting:
- Define the playing field with a cone.

Course:

- ▲4 starts the course and passes the ball to ▲2 into his running path (A).

- ▲1 makes a running feint towards the goal on the wing position (B), runs a curve, and receives a pass from ▲2 into his running path (C).

- ▲2 immediately moves back towards the side line after he played the pass (D).

- ▲1 dynamically dribbles along the defense line (E) and passes the ball to ▲4 (H). As soon as he passed the 7-meter line, he moves behind the defense line towards the 6-meter zone and stays there (J).

- If ●2 clearly steps forward (F) (E), ▲3 may receive a pass (G) (= **option 1**).

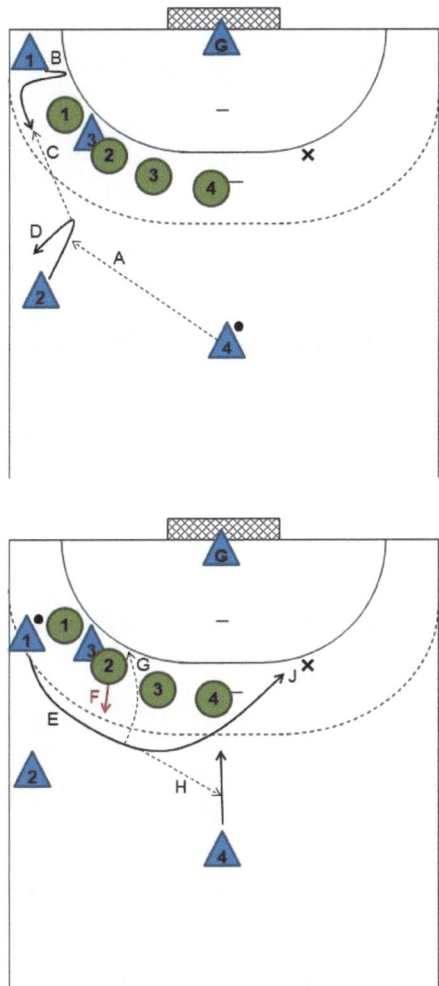

⚠ In the subsequent game, ▲1 keeps running until he reaches ●5 (not in the figure). The defense line on the left should be pulled apart through handing over/moving along (in order to avoid an outnumbered situation on the right side).

Handball Practice 14 – Interaction of back position players with the pivot – Shifting, Screening, and Using the Russian Screen

handball-uebungen.de
Trainingseinheiten und Übungen für Ihr Training!

- 4️⃣ makes a piston movement in direction of the goal and passes the ball (K) to 2️⃣ into his running path towards 2️⃣.

- 3️⃣ clearly places a screen next to 1️⃣ (L) who must not move around.

⚠️ 3️⃣ may use his body only for placing the screen; he must not use his hands (arms).

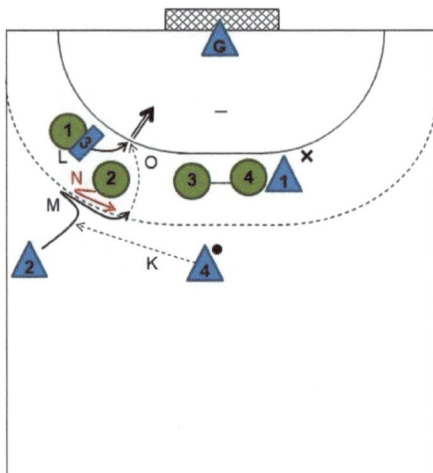

- 2️⃣ starts playing 1-on-1 against 2️⃣ in order to break through on the inner side (M and N).

⚠️ If 2️⃣ does not step out to interrupt the attack, 2️⃣ should make a jump shot or stem shot at the goal (= **option 2**). 2️⃣ may also break through during the 1-on-1 action (= **option 3**).

- If breaking through is not possible, 2️⃣ plays a bounce pass in direction of the goal zone. 3️⃣ leaves the screening position next to 1️⃣, runs towards the ball, and eventually shoots at the goal (O) (= **option 4**).
- Repeat the course on the other side after a few rounds.

No.: 5-8	Closing game	10	90

Setting:
- Make two teams. Both teams play 6-on-6 against each other.

Course:
- Both teams should start their attack with the wing player running along the defense line and the 1-on-1 action of 2️⃣ against 2️⃣.
- 3️⃣ should place a screen next to the wing player (mismatch) (see preparatory exercises).
- Afterwards, the attacking players may keep on playing "creatively".
- If they score a goal as a direct result of the screening (mismatch) action, this goal counts twice.
- Which team scores highest?

Handball Practice 14 – Interaction of back position players with the pivot – Shifting, Screening, and Using the Russian Screen

handball-uebungen.de
Trainingseinheiten und Übungen für Ihr Training!

5. About the editor

JÖRG MADINGER, born in Heidelberg (Germany) in 1970

July 2014 (further training): 3-day coaching workshop: "Basic components of goalkeeper training", held by the **German Handball Association (Deutscher Handballbund, DHB)**
Lecturers: Michael Neuhaus, Renate Schubert, Marco Stange, Norbert Potthoff, Olaf Gritz, Andreas Thiel, Henning Fritz

May 2014 (further training): 3-day coaching further training during the VELUX EHF Final4, held by the **German Handball Coaching Association (Deutsche Handball Trainer Vereinigung, DHTV)/DHB**
Lecturers: Jochen Beppler (DHB coach), Christian vom Dorff (DHB referee), Mark Dragunski (coach of TuSeM Essen, Germany), Klaus-Dieter Petersen (DHB coach), Manolo Cadenas (coach of the Spanish national team)

May 2013 (further training): 3-day coaching further training during the VELUX EHF Final4, held by the **DHTV/DHB**
Lecturers: Prof. Dr. Carmen Borggrefe (University of Stuttgart, Germany), Klaus-Dieter Petersen (DHB coach), Dr. Georg Froese (sports psychologist), Jochen Beppler (DHB base camp coach), Carsten Alisch (young talents' hockey coach)

Since July 2012: A-License, DHB

Since February 2011: Handball club trainings, coaching (training and competitive areas)

November 2011: Foundation of the Handball Specialist Publishing Company (Handball Fachverlag) (handall-uebungen.de, Handball Practice and Special Handball Practice)

May 2009: Foundation of the handball online platform handball-uebungen.de

2008-2010: Youth coordinator and youth coach, SG Leutershausen (Germany)

Since 2006: B-License

Editor's note
In 1995, a friend convinced me to join him in coaching a handball youth team (male, under 13 years of age).

This was the beginning of my career as a team handball coach. Ever since I enjoyed working as a coach and had high requirements concerning my exercises. Soon, the standard pool of exercises wasn't enough for me anymore and I started to modify and develop drills myself.

Today, I coach a broad range of youth and adult teams with different performance levels and adjust my training units to the individual needs of the teams.

A few years ago, I started selling my exercises and drills online at handball-uebungen.de. Since, in handball training, there is a tendency towards a general athletic training that focuses on coordination work – especially in the training of youth teams –, a large number of my games and exercises can be applied to other sports as well.

Get inspired by the various game concepts, be creative, and rely on your own experiences!

Yours sincerely,
Jörg Madinger

Handball Practice 14 – Interaction of back position players with the pivot – Shifting, Screening, and Using the Russian Screen

handball-uebungen.de
Trainingseinheiten und Übungen für Ihr Training!

6. Further reference books published by DV Concept

From warm-up to handball team play – 75 exercises for every handball training unit

By making your training units more diverse, you can increase the players' motivation, since you consistently offer new approaches to improve and refine familiar movement sequences. In this book, you will find inspiring exercises you can apply during each phase of your everyday team handball training – from warm-up and goalkeeper warm-up shooting to the common contents of the main phase and the closing games. Each exercise is illustrated and described in an easy, comprehensible manner. Specific notes give you tips on what you need to be aware of.

This book deals with the following key subjects:

Warm-up:
- Basic warm-up
- Short warm-up games
- Sprint contests
- Coordination
- Ball familiarization
- Goalkeeper warm-up shooting

Basic exercises, basic play, and target play:
- Offense/series of shots
- General offense
- Fast throw-off
- 1st and 2nd wave
- Defensive action
- Closing games
- Endurance

At the end of this book, you will find an entire methodological training unit. The objective of this training unit is to improve shooting and quick decision-making under pressure.

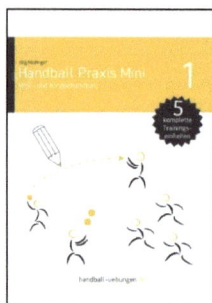

Minihandball training and handball training for young kids (5 training units)

Minihandball training and handball training for kids is different from handball training for older players and considerably different from handball training for competitive players. During their first contact with "handball", kids should be familiarized with the ball in a playful way. They should be taught that being active, doing sports, playing together, and even playing against each other is fun.

This book contains a short introduction to handball for kids and young children and its special characteristics as well as example exercises which help to make your training units interesting and more diverse.

Following this, there are five complete training units of different difficulty levels that focus on the basic handball techniques (dribbling, passing, catching, shooting, and defending in a game with opponents). The kids are playfully introduced to the subsequent handball-specific basics. At the same time, particular attention is payed to general physical experience and the development of coordination skills.

The exercises are illustrated and described in an easy, comprehensible manner. They can be immediately integrated in every training unit. By using the given training variants, you can easily adjust the difficulty level of the training units to the respective target group. The variants should also encourage you to modify and further develop the exercises to make each training unit a new and more diverse experience for the children.

Handball Practice 14 – Interaction of back position players with the pivot – Shifting, Screening, and Using the Russian Screen

handball-uebungen.de
Trainingseinheiten und Übungen für Ihr Training!

Passing and catching while moving – 60 exercises for each handball training unit

Passing and catching are two basic handball techniques which must be trained and improved continuously. These 60 practical exercises offer you various options to train passing and catching in a challenging and diverse manner. The exercises particularly focus on improving passing and catching skills even during highly dynamic movements. The drills therefore combine new running paths and movements similar to real game situations.

The exercises are illustrated and described in an easy, comprehensible manner. They can be immediately integrated in every training unit. Various difficulty and complexity levels allow for adjustment of the passing and catching drills to each age group.

Effective goalkeeper warm-up shooting – 60 exercises for every handball unit

Goalkeeper warm-up shooting is essential for almost every training unit. These 60 warm-up shooting exercises provide you with a variety of ideas to make the warm-up shooting challenging and diverse, both for the goalkeepers and the field players. The exercises particularly focus on improving the players' dynamics even during the warm-up shooting.

The exercises are illustrated and described in an easy, comprehensible manner. They can be immediately integrated in every training unit. Whether you combine the exercises with additional coordination drills or use them as an introduction to the main part – various difficulty levels allow for adjustment of the warm-up shooting to each training unit and age group.

Handball Practice 14 – Interaction of back position players with the pivot – Shifting, Screening, and Using the Russian Screen

handball-uebungen.de
Trainingseinheiten und Übungen für Ihr Training!

Competitive games for your everyday handball training – 60 exercises for each age-group
Handball needs quick and correct decisions in each game situation. This can be trained playfully and diversely through handball-specific games. These 60 exercises are divided into seven categories and train the playing skills.

The book deals with the following subjects:
- Team ball variants
- Team play with different targets
- Tag games
- Sprint and relay race games
- Ball throwing and transportation games
- Games from other types of sports
- Complex closing game variants

The exercises are illustrated and described in an easy, comprehensible manner. They can be immediately integrated in every training unit. Various difficulty levels, additional notes, and possible variations allow for adjustment to each age group.

Paperback from the Handball Practice series (Handball Praxis) (five training units each)

Handball Practice 11 – Extensive and diverse athletics training

For further reference and e-books visit us at:

www.handball-uebungen.de

www.ingramcontent.com/pod-product-compliance
Lightning Source LLC
Chambersburg PA
CBHW042129080426
42735CB00001B/21